D1302733

Signs
and
Spaces

Organized by
DK Holland
Roger Whitehouse
Stephan Geissbuhler
Deborah Sussman

Written by
J. Abbott Miller

Essays by
J. Abbott Miller
Alan Fletcher
Deborah Sussman
Takenobu Igarashi
Wim Crouwel

Designed by
Whitehouse & Company

Published by
Rockport/Allworth Editions
Rockport Publishers, Inc.
Allworth Press

Signs
and
Spaces

R|A

DISTRIBUTED BY NORTH LIGHT BOOKS · CINCINNATI, OHIO

9686.2
M615s

Project Director:
DK Holland,
Lewin/Holland, Inc.
Book Designer:
Roger Whitehouse,
Whitehouse & Company
Writer:
J. Abbott Miller
Copy Editor:
Philip F. Clark
Production Manager:
Lindsey Payne,
Whitehouse & Company
Printer:
Regent, Hong Kong

Copyright ©1994 by
Rockport Publishers,
Inc., and Allworth
Press

All rights reserved.
No part of this book
may be reproduced in
any form without
written permission of
the copyright owners.
All images in this book
have been reproduced
with the knowledge
and prior consent of
the designers concerned
and no responsibility
is accepted by the
producer, publisher
or printer for any
infringement of copy-
right or otherwise
arising from the
contents of this
publication. Every
effort has been made
to ensure that credits
accurately comply
with information
supplied. All images
and photographs on
pages58-65 are copyright
© Disney and no
reproductions may be
made without the
express written
authorization of The
Walt Disney Company.

First published in the
United States by
Rockport Allworth
Editions, a trade
name of Rockport
Publishers, Inc. and
Allworth Press.

Rockport Publishers, Inc.
146 Granite Street
Rockport,
Massachusetts 01966
Telephone: 508/546-9590
Facsimile: 508/546-7141
Telex: 51886019284
ROCKPORT PUB

Allworth Press
10 East 23rd Street
New York, NY 10010
Telephone: 212/777-8395
Facsimile: 212/777-8261

Distribution to the book
and art trade in the
United States and Canada
by: North Light Books,
an imprint of:
F&W Publications
1507 Dana Avenue
Cincinnati, Ohio 45207
Telephone:
513/531-2222

Distributed to the book
and art trade throughout
the rest of the world by:
Rockport Publishers, Inc.
Rockport, Massachusetts
01966

ISBN: 1-56496-031-5
Printed in Hong Kong

Table of Contents

Acknowledgments

It was Tad Crawford of Allworth Press who conceived of the idea of a series of books of the work of graphic designers. The first book is named *Graphic Design: New York– The Work of 39 Great Graphic Design Firms from the City That Put Graphic Design on the Map*. This book's success in creating a high visibility for graphic design led us to conceive of *Graphic Design: America–The Work of Twenty-eight Design Firms from Across the United States and Canada* and *Signs and Spaces–A Survey of the Environmental Graphic Design Work of Twenty-two Major International Design Firms*. Tad had the vision to include Rockport Publishers as co-publishers of the book. Rockport Publishers Stan Patey, Don Traynor and Marta Schooler lent their invaluable publishing and sales expertise and wisdom throughout the project.

The firms contributing to this book were carefully selected by an editorial board consisting of Deborah Sussman, Stephan Geissbuhler, and Roger Whitehouse. After the firm selections were made, each firm was basically free to choose what projects were to be shown.

Thanks to the Society for Environmental Graphic Design. It was the SEGD membership directory that made it possible for us to contact virtually all the designers we decided to invite into the book. In gratitude to the fine work of the SEGD, the designers in the book have agreed to contribute all royalties due to them for this project to SEGD's Education Fund. SEGD, can be contacted at: One Story Street Cambridge, MA 02138 Telephone: 617/868-3381 Facsimile: 617/868-3591

Regent Printing artfully placed ink on paper, making Whitehouse & Company's meticulous mechanicals worthwhile.

Finally and naturally, our greatest thanks go to the 22 firms who had the vision, talent and confidence necessary to create this compendium.

We are indebted to J. Abbott Miller for articulating his views on the discipline of environ-mental graphic design. Philip F. Clark, our able copy editor, was tireless and without complaint in working on impossible deadlines.

E.J. Gallegos of Lewin/Holland, Inc. helped run interference when communications started to get bogged down, keeping lines open with all the firms in the book. A round of applause goes to Lindsey Payne, of Whitehouse & Company, who managed the production of the book from start to finish without losing, even for a second, her good sense of humor, humanity or dedication to perfection.

About This Book

Signs and Spaces is a book that couldn't be more timely. In fact, in the past decade environmental graphic design has finally emerged as a clearly-defined profession, its members recruited from the ranks of graphic designers, product designers, interior designers, and architects.

In l990, a series of books on the work of graphic designers was conceived. The objective was to expose the viewing public to the highest standard of excellence in design. The series was started with two books, *Graphic Design: New York* and *Graphic Design: America*, both organized by DK Holland, Michael Bierut and William Drenttel. The success of these first books (*Graphic Design: New York* went into a second printing within six months of publication) has been fuel for the continuation of the series.

Signs and Spaces is the first book to focus on a specific discipline within graphic design. Environmental graphic design is unique as an area of concentration. Its ability to mature into a distinct profession, has very much been due, in the USA in particular, to the founding of SEGD, the Society for Environmental Graphic Design, whose annual conferences both inspire and act as an arena for the interchange of both creative and technical ideas.

Choosing the design firms to be invited into the book was, in one way, very difficult, in another, very simple. None of us had seen the entire portfolios of most of the firms that were asked; that made it difficult to envision the book as a whole until it was actually completed. Concerned with the book's

integrity and balance, we took pains to search for worthy designers to form an eclectic mix; small and large firms, traditionalists and experimentalists. Some very talented firms did not make the invitation list because they were generalists without a comprehensive portfolio in the area of environmental graphic design. It's important to note that most environmental graphic design is created by firms that also work on publications, promotion or packaging: there are very few pure environmental graphic design firms.

The 22 firms included in the book were asked to create a complete picture of the scope of their work for the reader.

Signs and Spaces has been very satisfying to work on. A community of designers exists and it's a joy to celebrate that fact. It's clear from this book that there is a myriad of exceptional talent in the world ready, willing and able to design our public spaces. The more the public and private sectors allow designers to push the envelope, the more the public's design awareness will be enriched. Public spaces are where the people learn about graphic design. Environmental graphic design is the art of the people.

DK Holland
Roger Whitehouse
Stephan Geissbuhler
Deborah Sussman

December 1993

By J. Abbott Miller

The Architecture of Information

From *2001: A Space Odyssey*, Photograph © Keir Dullea 1968/ Motion Picture & Television Archive.

From *Barbarella* to *2001*, the environment of the future–at least as envisioned by Hollywood–is made of walls that conceal a mass of information beneath their deceptively simple surfaces. TV screens, numerical displays, and spigots for Space Age cocktails are accessed by the touch of a button; sleek plexiglass sheaths disclose devices for communication and pleasure. This image of the future is indebted to the kitchens and bathrooms of the 1930s, which sought to envelop a range of equipment within a smooth continuum of porcelain enamel, Formica laminate, and Monel metal. Reaching its popular pinnacle in the 1950s, this smooth-surfaced world was conceived by packaging and advertising designers like Raymond Loewy, whose streamlined locomotives and modern-istic interiors of the 1930s translated aero-dynamic theory onto immobile objects and environments; in the '60s, Loewy would design zero-gravity toilet facilities for a Space Age come true.

Using expensive materials and processes, contemporary signage often emulates the seamless ideal of the Space Age interior, with its equipment and information seamlessly merged with the skin of the environment. The inscrutably immaterial monolith in *2001* resembles an expensive corporate lobby directory–staggeringly well produced, but what is it? One overriding feature of the Space Age dream is that the environment of the future is so meticulously planned in advance that nothing needs to be bluntly attached after-the-fact. In these post-mechanical environments, things are not connected with rivets or bolts, since they are already organically linked to the building. The only moment of contact between information and the viewer is when a message offers itself through a shiny VDT or quartz display, or through a small slit from which a tidy scrap of paper propels itself towards the user. (An exception to this fantasy of a seamless future is the brilliantly anachronistic view of high-tech offered by the 1985 movie *Brazil*.)

Human encounters are increasingly mediated by sophisticated information devices: from such consumer products as fax machines, cellular phones, and paging beepers to commercially-based interfaces such as cash machines, drive-in fast-food windows, and home shopping networks. Design prophets speculate that the homes and offices of the not-so-distant-future will be equipped not with a few centralized communications appliances (phone, television, computer) but rather with a dispersed network of tiny devices, disseminated across every facet of a user's life, from car to garden, from bedroom to basement.

The so-called "smart house" of tomorrow will be characterized not by its architecture, properly speaking, but by small-scale gadgets and the information systems to which they are wired. This futurist scenario is, of course, already here in the humble form of electronically programmed VCRs, coffee pots, clock radios, and sprinkler systems. Theorists of post-Modernism such as Jean Baudrillard and Jean-Francois Lyotard have taught us to think of our social world as an endless series of texts: the contemporary consumer landscape of flickering LED displays is making real this information-based understanding of culture.

The term "information overload", which has been used to describe the proliferation of publishing and media, may be equally applied to the physical environment. Environmental graphic designers have the task of making social space more legible. It is by now accepted practice that the work of such designers should respond to architectural and social context. This is why the term "environmental graphics" is largely supplanting "signage". The former suggests a careful merging of information with its context, inviting associations of ecology and preservation. The term signage, by comparison, suggests a ready-made object, such as the stamped metal numbers and

J. Abbott Miller is the director of Design Writing Research, *a studio founded upon the relationship between words and pictures. He is the co-author of* The Bathroom, The Kitchen, and the Aesthetics of Waste: A Process of Elimination, *and* The ABC's of ▲■●: The Bauhaus and Design Theory. *His articles have appeared in* Print, Eye, Emigré, *and* Zone. *His studio creates exhibitions, books, magazines, and environmental graphics.*

fluorescent signs sold in hardware stores.

This emerging semantic distinction serves to separate a professionally-defined and theoretically self-conscious practice from a more strictly commercial one. The Society for Environmental Graphic Design (SEGD), in hoping to establish a more solid ground from which designers can operate, uses the term environmental graphics to suggest an integrated approach to the problem of weaving verbal and visual information into the fabric of buildings and spaces. Yet despite the aspiration shared by the best practitioners to integrate signs with their settings, most clients, designers, and users view signs as detachable labels, analogous to the captions next to pictures.

Like a picture, the building, park, or subway station is seen as the complete, self-contained work, while the sign–like a caption– is seen as conveying extrinsic, non-essential information. This model positions the social usage of environments as something added after the fact: signs are what get tacked on after the architect or builder is "done." (Of course, graphic designers sometimes invert this myth by treating buildings as containers

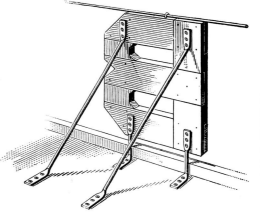

Illustration of a wooden roof-mounted sign, secured with angle irons. From *Elements of Lettering and Sign Painting*, The Collier Engineer Company, 1899.

Inscription on the facade
of S. Maria Novella, Florence,
by Alberti. Commisioned
in 1457-1458.

for signs.) The philosophy behind environmental graphics is to view social usage as *generative*, not *secondary*, to the evolution of buildings; signs should therefore be part of planning from the beginning.

As Reyner Banham has pointed out in his 1972 book *The Well-Tempered Environment*, architectural history has denied the primacy of HVAC technologies to the design of buildings. Information systems also have been suppressed from official aesthetic history, where graphics appear only occasionally as a concern for the serious architect. A notable exception is found in the work of Leon Battista Alberti, who, as the paradigmatic "Renaissance man," concerned himself with all aspects of the arts and sciences, from poetry and philosophy to painting, perspective, architecture, and even, the design of letters. Alberti's commitment to reviving the architecture of the "ancients" extended to monumental inscriptions, as seen, for example, in his design for the Tempio Maletestiano, built in Mantua in the 1450s. Here, Alberti adapted a Roman triumphal arch to the facade of an existing Christian church; the text carved across the architrave consists of meticulously designed capitals based on Roman carvings.

Alberti's use of classical inscriptions in this and other church designs, including S. Maria Novella in Florence, fed the humanist fashion for classical calligraphy in the production of manuscripts and, later, the taste for "Roman" type in printed books. Elegant capitals carved into monumental public buildings have remained a staple of classical architecture, enduring across numerous revivals of Greco-Roman styles in the nineteenth century; carved Roman capitals remain today a stately signifier for such modern "temples" as museums, libraries, and banks.

One of the most spectacular reinventions of the monumental classical inscription is found in the Bibliothèque Ste.-Geneviève, designed in Paris in 1843 by Henri Labrouste. Columns of authors' names are written on the stone exterior of this grand public library; the positioning of the text on the outside of the building directly mirrors the placement of the shelves of books inside. Labrouste, who embraced classicism as an architectural language that solemnly reflects structure, here used monumental letters to map the interior content of a building onto its exterior shell. In a concise merging of social function and public image, Labrouste gave material form to the link between architecture and literature.

ODBEFHIJKLMN
PQURSTVWCG
QU WA &YXZJ

Alphabet for the London Underground by Edward Johnston, 1916.

The carved capitals of the Trajan column were the inspiration behind the thoroughly twentieth-century letters which Edward Johnston designed for the London Underground in 1916.

Johnston's alphabet, which became the basis of his student Eric Gill's font Gill Sans in 1929, was at the heart of an early example of "environmental graphics" as we understand it today: a complete program of wayfinding devices, from permanent signs to printed maps and schedules to promotional advertising–in short, a total system enabling users to navigate a complex space and giving a memorable identity to the organization responsible for it. In contrast to the spectacular, lushly organic Art Nouveau subway kiosks of the Paris Metro,

Paris Metro kiosk
designed by
Hector Guimard
circa 1900.

designed by Hector Guimard circa 1900, the graphics of the London Underground strove to advance a rational view of the city and its uses.

The design of the New York City subway system is famed neither for its systematic rigor nor its ornamental flamboyance, yet early in its history its makers engaged in the theory of wayfinding. An article in *House and Garden*, published shortly before the system opened in 1904, uses terms that remain resonant today to describe the need for geographic cues in a placeless, underground environment:"...how the rider in a Subway...may know under what portion of the city he is speeding is the matter which concerns us here. It is a mistake to assume that in traversing a city a person locates himself by the names or numbers of the streets alone. Rather is it the buildings, or other striking landmarks, which alone catch the eye and bring the passenger from his seat in time to alight at the proper moment from the surrounding elevated car.... But how is the traveler underground to be provided with such aids? Only by a difference in the design of the stations and the method of placing signs upon them." (*House and Garden*, Vol. V No. 2, February 1904:96-7.)

Architects Heins & La Farge were hired by the Rapid Transit Commission to design the new subway stations. The techniques they devised to distinguish one underground stop from another include variations in the color and shape of sign cartouches and the attempt to match an eclectic palette of styles and motifs to different regions of the city. For example, the designers employed "sturdy forms" and "restraint of ornament" in the "workaday heart" of the downtown office district, while using Dutch tulips to invoke the early settlers

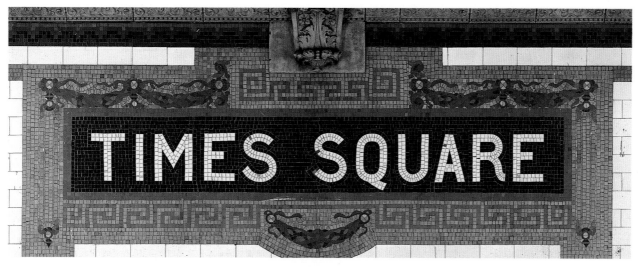

Times Square ceramic tile, photograph ©David Lubarsky 1993.

of Bleecker Street. Station signs were designed to merge with the supporting wall by sinking into its surface: the panels are made "of dull blue faïence with letters in a corresponding artistic dull white," a material of "indestructibility and permanence" that "can be built several inches into the wall and becomes part of it."

The New York subway is now associated chiefly with the brightly rational system of train line identifiers designed by Vignelli and Associates in the mid-1970s– a flat graphic code superimposed over the background of urban dirt, steel girders, and dusty donut shops. Yet the original elements of the city's ceramic subway signage remain largely intact today, scarred as they are by nearly a century of grime, crime, and abuse. While this subway system is commonly denigrated–by users and non-users alike–as one of the ugliest and scariest in the world, it remains an integral part of one of the largest mass transit networks in America, functioning in one of the nation's few metropolitan regions to offer viable alternatives to car commuting.

While a subway system is marked by the dispersion, lack of center, and fundamental "betweenness" that characterizes a telephone network, the office tower–another prototypically modern design form–is a centralized monument. Yet in addition to being a properly architectural object, a modern office building is also a device for managing communications. An early example of an office building conceived of as a complex information system is Frank Lloyd Wright's Larkin Building, built in Buffalo in 1904. Serving as the headquarters for a mail-order soap company, the Larkin Building was designed to accommodate a vast flow of paperwork: receiving orders, arranging shipments, coordinating inventory, etc. Charged with navigating this river of information was a clerical force consisting of more than a thousand employees, most of them young women.

Wright designed every aspect of the building, from its exterior and interior architecture to its heating systems and furniture. The sequencing of the rooms and structure of the desks were all conceived to maximize efficiency through physical and emotional control. Seeking to enhance the worker's productivity, Wright designed inspirational messages that are printed in gold letters on the walls lining the vast inner atrium, listing such virtues as *INTELLIGENCE, ENTHUSIASM, CONTROL* and *GENEROSITY, ALTRUISM, SACRIFICE.*

An article published in the company's house organ, *The Larkin Idea*, in 1907, explained the poetic strategy of these signs:

"Simple words are inscribed rather than great quotations because they permit independence of thought and individuality of interpretation. A great thought once said in words, however aptly put, is like a carved image; it is accepted as complete by all but the closest reasoners. A simple word is suggestive; it is a text for the exercise of reason and the imagination." (Reprinted in Jack Quinan, *Frank Lloyd Wright's Larkin Building, Myth and Fact*, MIT Press, 1987.)

Thus graphic texts were incorporated into a complete information environment that sought to mold the minds and bodies of its users.

The avant-garde artists and designers of the 1920s designed numerous projects which combine architecture and graphics. Educational exhibitions designed by El Lissitzky sought to educate an international public about the social and economic progress of the young Soviet Union; he used large-scale photography and dramatic lettering to generate emotionally charged settings, replacing the traditional focus of exhibitions on *objects* with a focus on *texts*. Gustav Klutsis, another Soviet artist, created kiosk designs that combine graphic messages with radio technology, supported by structures drawn from the language of engineering. Following the work of the Constructivists, Herbert Bayer designed news kiosks during his tenure at the Bauhaus. Commercial rather than propagandistic in their function, Bayer's proposed kiosks exceeded the technological possibilities of the 1920s: one design suggests the use of sound, light, projected film images, and even smoke, used to write a product's name in thin air. Bayer's theoretical diagram depicting the ideal exhibition as a total information environment, enveloping the viewer in multi-faceted planes of image and text, has influenced many subsequent designers.

Apart from a few "legitimate" experiments with graphics by architects, artists, and designers, signage has largely belonged to the ephemeral domains of advertising and commercial art. Until the 1950s, the ubiquitous world of everyday signs was largely dismissed by "serious" designers and by the cultural custodians of "good design" until it was rediscovered by the Pop movements in New York and London. From Andy Warhol to

Inscriptions in the Larkin Building, Buffalo, by Frank Lloyd Wright, 1904. Reprinted by permission of the Buffalo and Erie County Historical Society.

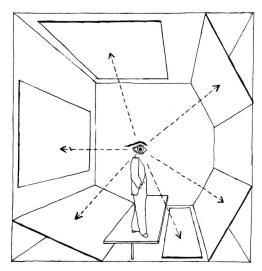

Drawing of "inclusive picture of all possibilities" by Hebert Bayer, 1939. Published in *PM*, vol. VI, No. 2 (December-January, 1939-1940).

Richard Hamilton, young artists reveled in the trash of the "commercial vernacular"– Hollywood films, Detroit cars, and neon signs. The Pop revolution found its way back into the discourse of high architecture through the writing and teaching of Robert Venturi and Denise Scott Brown, whose 1972 book *Learning from Las Vegas* shocked the community of third-generation Modernists by redefining architecture as *sign*. With their famous diagram of the duck and the decorated shed, Venturi and Scott Brown celebrated the model of building that had come to characterize suburban shopping districts: the blank, concrete box whose meaning, function, and ornament is derived from the signs connected to it, whether attached to the top of the building or standing beckoning across the parking lot to the highway.

Environmental graphics occupies the border between a variety of cultural practices: from the "professions" of graphic design, industrial design, and architecture, to the "trades" of commercial art, advertising, and real estate development, to the civic sciences of zoning, planning, and building codes.

The emergence of environmental graphics as a distinct field of design points to the centrality of *verbal* rather than *visual* language to contemporary culture. This book documents the designers who have participated in the formation of this new discipline, which is pieced together out of diverse aspects of culture and diverse fields of knowledge.

The "Long Island Duck" referred to by Venturi, Rauch, and Scott-Brown in their 1972 book *Learning from Las Vegas.* Photograph ©John Margolies/Esto, 1979.

Lance Wyman, Ltd.

118 West 80th Street
New York, NY 10024
212/580-3010

Principal:
Lance Wyman

Year Founded: 1979
Size of Firm: 5

Lance Wyman and design associate Peter Murdoch were selected through an international competition to design the graphics for the 1968 Summer Olympic Games in Mexico City. They collaborated on the design of the wayfinding stations and directional signage.

Lance Wyman, principal of Lance Wyman, Ltd.

Wyman created the "Mexico '68" logotype which includes the five Olympic rings, the year, and the city's name. The radiating parallel-line typography was used in a variety of applications. This graphic motif refers to pre-Hispanic and contemporary Mexican graphic forms.

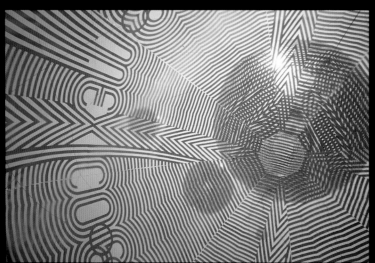

In designing the signs and symbol system for the 1968 Olympic games in Mexico, Lance Wyman was inspired by art forms indigenous to Mexico. The system included the official logotype, and a series of pictograms for each of the sports and cultural events, which functioned as an effective international visual language, comprehensible to all visitors not fluent in the required official languages of Spanish, English and French. The system was applied to the directional signage and wayfinding stations, events tickets, stamps, advertising and collateral print materials, posters and publications.

Key Clients:
American Museum of
Natural History,
CaminoReal Hotel,
City of Calgary,
City of Edmonton,
Merrill Lynch,
Mexico City Metro,
Minnesota Zoo,
Monterrey Museum of
Contemporary Art,
National Zoological
Park, Newark
International
Airport, "Papalote"
Children's Museum
of Mexico City,
Rockefeller Center,
Shearson/American
Express, Skidmore,
Owings & Merrill,
Smithsonian Institution,
The Methodist Hospital,
XIX Olympiad in
Mexico City, Toronto
Transit Commission,
U.S. Postal Service,
Washington D.C.
Transit Authority,
UNICEF.

Lance Wyman, Ltd.

Directional signage for
the Mexico City Metro
included internally
illuminated pylon signs
on which pictograms,
expressing points of
interest, identified each
station. The "M" logo
refers to the initial three
lines of the rail system.

Lance Wyman's work for museums, transit systems, airports, office buildings and other public spaces over the past 30 years has helped define the field of environmental graphics. A former director of the Society for Environmental Graphic Design (SEGD), and currently president of its Education Foundation, Wyman began his career in the early '60s, when corporate identity and the ideal of a completely designed environment were just beginning to be tested. After working with George Nelson as an exhibition designer, Wyman pursued a series of ambitious projects in Mexico. As Director of Graphic Design for the 1968 Olympic Games in Mexico City, he created a system of international pictographs, which he combined with a custom typeface based on traditional Mexican folk art. A similar sensibility of rational modernism tempered with playful wit animates numerous other projects that have explored the possibilities of pictorial and typographic communication at an urban scale.

Stamps depicting sports
events pictograms
for the Munich Summer
and Sapporo Winter
Olympic Games.

Blue-and-white porcelain
enamel banners
suspended from
lampposts along the
Washington Mall depict
the symbols of the
Smithsonian Institution
museums and other
national monuments.
Three-dimensional

location maps of cast
polyresin are housed in
kiosks constructed in the
architectural style of
the Smithsonian Castle.
Design: Wyman &
Cannan; Design Directors:
Lance Wyman, Bill
Cannan; Assistant
Designers: Brian Flahive,
Tucker Viemeister,
Tom DeMonse, Francisco
Gallardo; Architects:
Skidmore, Owings &
Merrill, Washington, D.C.

Trash receptacles also serve to direct visitors to zoo stations and accommodations.

Cast stone Zoo logotype entrance sign incorporates the same squared "O" used throughout the system.

For the Smithsonian Institution's National Zoological Park in Washington D.C., Wyman and Cannan created a unified program of signage and wayfinding graphics, which includes cast stone and porcelain enameled "totems" leading visitors to specific species areas. Visitors follow pathways indicated by animal paw tracks leading to each area.
Design Directors: Lance Wyman, Bill Cannan; Assistant Designers: Brian Flahive, Tucker Viemeister, Tom de Monse, Ernesto Lehfeld; Architects: Fryer & Vanderpool.

The five major exhibit areas or trails for the Minnesota Zoo are identified by numerals, each of which incorporates the symbol of an animal of that area or trail. "Guide bird" directional arrows appear on all interior and exterior pedestrian signs as well as those for vehicular traffic. Design Director: Lance Wyman; Assistant Designers: Linda Iskander, Stephen Schlott; Architects: Interdesign, Inc.; Fabricator: Heritage Display.

A sculptural application for "Papalote," the Children's Museum in Mexico City. The symbol includes shapes inspired by the forms of the museum's buildings designed by architect Ricardo Legorreta.

The moose logo for the Minnesota Zoo translated into a cast stone entrance monolith.

A wayfinding system of pylons and sign panels incorporate "Guide bird" directional arrows, animal number symbols and service pictographs to help pedestrians and vehicles find their way.

Sculpture becomes architecture in the
sign system created for the Museo
de Arte Contemporaneo (MARCO)
in Monterrey, Nuevo Leon, Mexico.
For the museum's entrance sign, stone
letterforms emerge from the wall into a
squared "O" suggesting the museum's
central patio design. Banners and wall
signposts have cut-outs whose shadows
mirror this box-in-a-square design.

Promotional print
materials utilize square
die-cut and foldout to
refer to the museum's
architectural shape.

Stone rings found in pre-Hispanic ball courts inspired the design of the museum's wall signposts.

The museum's reception station reiterates the stone letterform used in the entrance sign. Graphic Design Director: Lance Wyman; Assistant Designers: Denise Guerra, Linda Iskander; Architect: Legorreta Arquitectos.

Blackfoot Indian tepees were traditionally adorned with a series of bold white circles representing star patterns. Navigation by stars' positions in the sky was a Blackfoot method of finding directions to points on the compass. The "+15" logo was developed from these patterns.

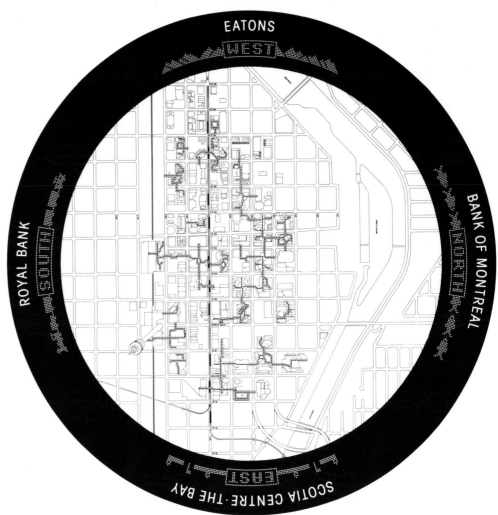

The "+15" system in Calgary, Alberta, Canada is a climate-controlled pedestrian environment developed within an elevated system of walkway bridges 15 feet above street level. Its symbol, a man in a white Stetson walking across a formation of circles, is based on traditional Blackfoot Indian tepee designs and the traditional hat of Calgary. The circles are used throughout the system on the floors of open spaces and corridors, and act as directional paths to connecting bridges.

The grid map of the complete "+15" system indicates the many destinations and connecting bridges in the pedestrian walkway. The four compass points are visually represented by corresponding geographic Calgary landmarks: Bow River trout in the North, the Canadian Rockies in the West, The Canadian Pacific Railway train in the South and Fort Calgary in the East. Design Director: Lance Wyman; Assistant Designers: Mark Fuller, Linda Iskander, Rob Roehrick, Stacey Wyman; Consulting Architect: Peter Haley; Fabrication: Chinook Plastics Ltd.

The City of Edmonton's Pedway is a tri-level pedestrian walkway system. The Pedway logo, in three bars of color, indicates the various levels with a "walking" pictogram.

American Museum of Natural History

Computer-generated floor maps can be updated by the museum staff as needed. Visitors can use the maps throughout the separate exhibition areas. The maps provide individual layouts of each floor and the corresponding floor icons.

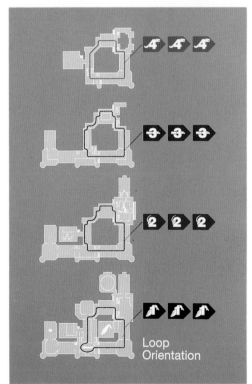

Loop Orientation

The signage system for the Museum of Natural History in New York integrates the floor numbers with visual wayfinding icons, using them on all directories and signs. Directional floor markers appear along the base of walls to mark orientation loops on each exhibit floor. The logo for the system is based on the original architecture of the building's tower shape. Design Director: Lance Wyman; Assistant Designers: Denise Guerra, Linda Iskander, Ralph Hertle; Photography: AMNH, Denis Finnin, Craig Chesek; Fabrication: M.T. Fuller.

Each of the museum's floor numbers graphically relates to one of the exhibitions on that floor; dinosaurs, North American birds, African mammals and ocean life. "Zero" for the lower level, where the restaurants are located, is represented by a table setting.

**Hellmuth, Obata &
Kassabaum, Inc.**

1831 Chestnut Street
St. Louis, MO 63103
314/421-2000

Principals:
Gyo Obata,
Co-Chairman
Jerome Sincoff,
Co-Chairman,
President and CEO
King Graf,
Vice Chairman
Charles P. Reay,
Director, Exhibition
and Graphic Design

Year Founded: 1956
Size of Firm: 1000

Plants and man are
joined in the symbol
for the Missouri
Botanical Garden.

Exhibits define the
ecological crisis and
suggest how we might
better care for the earth.

Mediterranean House

…dentity, and signage
of Mediterranean House
exhibit, designed for
the Missouri Botanical
Garden, St. Louis.
Utilizing transparent
and highly reflective
surface materials, HOK
was able to implement
an extensive, yet
harmonious signage
system throughout
the garden. Craw
Clarendon type unifies
the separate signage
elements. Designers:
Charles P. Reay,
Ed Bydalek,
Margaret Coates.

The "Jungle of the Apes"
exhibit designed for
the St. Louis Zoo
developed the signage
displays as an educa-
tional environment. All
the images in the painted
steel and enamel infor-
mation panels were
actually reproduced in
the enamel-making
process, simulating four-
color photography.
Designers: Charles P.
Reay, Louise W. Angst,
Theresa Henrekin,
Bevin Grant; Fabricators:
Enameltec, Langley,
ASI Sign Systems,
Don Asbee Metal Studio.

Key Clients:
Missouri
Botanical Garden,
Exxon Corporation,
The Florida Aquarium,
The Federal
Reserve Bank,
Gerald D. Hines Interests,
IBM,
Kellogg Company,
King Khaled
International Airport,
King Saud University,
Levi Strauss
and Company,
Metropolitan Life
Insurance Company,
Mobil Oil Corporation,
The Smithsonian
Institution,
St. Louis Union Station-
The Rouse Company,
St. Louis
Zoological Park,
United States
Government General
Services Administration.

Hellmuth, Obata & Kassabaum, Inc.

 Hellmuth, Obata & Kassabaum, Inc.'s design of the 10,000-square foot exhibition at "The Living World" at the St. Louis Zoo exemplifies the convergence of education, spectacle and entertainment at a modern zoological park. "The Living World" joins living things with high tech in an expansive, multi-level celebration of the richness and diversity of the natural world. The firm's graphic design work parallels the breadth of its architectural practice: corporate facilities, airports, hotels, commercial, retail, and mixed use centers, museums and educational institutions, universities, hospitals, and entertainment and leisure facilities. For the corporate headquarters of the Kellogg Company, HOK translated a stylized image of wheat into designs in bronze, wood, glass and textiles; and the wholesome symbol is reiterated in the company's impressive art collection. For the Levi-Strauss corporate headquarters, HOK reflected the company's essence by designing environmental signage with the famous blue jeans button emblazoned on mirrored plaques.

For the Levi Strauss San Francisco corporate headquarters, a magnified brass jean button was used as the company's symbol. The brass button is also mounted on chrome-plated brass backgrounds for other site signage. The plaques are floated in glass. The building names, set in Clarendon type, are photo-etched in the chrome background and filled with a "bluejeans blue" colored enamel. Designer: Charles P. Reay.

The mirrored surfaced
signs reflect the garden
at the heart of the Plaza.

Hellmuth, Obata & Kassabaum, Inc.

Polished bronze letters are mounted upon epoxy clad cast concrete forms which interpret the Saint Louis Galleria's logo and identify the project.

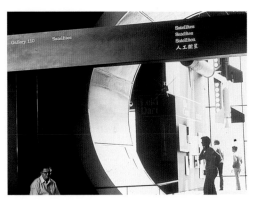

The National Air and Space Museum, Smithsonian Institution, is the single most popular cultural institution in the world. Multilingual signing directs its millions of annual visitors and reinforces an impression of the world-wide significance of the objects in the museum's collections and the achievements/events they represent. Craw Clarendon, the chosen typographic family, was selected for its appropriateness to the character of both the architecture of the building and The Smithsonian Institution. Galleries are identified by internally illuminated signs which span their entries.

The museum's symbol, in bronze, is set as a compass rose in the floor of the central gallery, in front of the Apollo 11 Capsule and the Wright's Flyer.

A pineapple, the symbol of hospitality, was the genesis of the design of the sculptural elements which, in pairs, form the gateways that flank the drives into the Galleria, a two-million-square-foot retail center in suburban St. Louis. Twenty eight feet tall, they are fabricated of cast concrete and fiberglass. Concealed fluorescent lights illuminate the crowns. Inside the mall, the directories (above) are made of polished bronze and epoxy coated steel. The obelisk form is common to all freestanding signing.

Hellmuth, Obata & Kassabaum, Inc.

An autoanimatronic figure of Charles Darwin greets visitors to the exhibits at "The Living World". HOK has made frequent use of entertainment technologies to assure the accessibility of the exhibits.

Much of the signage for the Zoo is designed around a curved format. The typeface Gill Sans, in metal, was used for its flexibility to be modified to the different weights and sizes of the curved display.

The fiberglass directory to "The Living World" is mounted to a steel and glass handrail.

To create a broadened perspective for the educational purpose of zoos, HOK's designs for "The Living World", a new pavilion at the St. Louis Zoo, draw upon the fantastic so as to bring a sense of wonder and celebration into the institution's signage program. Large fiberglass bas-relief sculptures on The Living World's facades, and letter forms expressed in the patterns of animal skins reflect the diversity of life to be found in the building's exhibits. Designers: Charles P. Reay, Louise Angst, Cicely Drennan, Theresa Henrekin; Fabricators: Crampton Inc., ASI Sign.

An engaging gargoyle, this fiberglass sculpture, a Jackson's Chameleon, keeps an eye on visitors entering "The Living World."

Bas-relief terra-cotta
panels with forms
inspired by grains,
braided breads and food-
stuffs frame the entries
to all office areas.

Triangular bronze forms
are designed in a
tapestry of sea-of-wheat
in a sculptured wall
in the reception area.

For the Kellogg Company's corporate
headquarters in Battle Creek, Michigan,
HOK took the cereal company's mainstay
image and turned what could have been
a cliche into a contemporary symbol of
universal good health. The design program
utilized imagery themes of harvest, good
health and prosperity. A diverse use of
crafts was a major component of the
program. Architectural ornamentation in
polished bronze, wood, etched and leaded
glass, and textiles all have been patterned
with a stylized wheat motif. "The genesis
of all the interior design was found
in expressing Kellogg's connections to
the land," explain the designers.

In the servery of the corporate dining facility, forged iron ornamentation and patterns in wall tile suggest specific foods. Designers: Gyo Obata, Charles P. Reay; Project Designers: Kathy Gregory, Cicely Drennan, Debby Fitzpatrick, Louise Angst, Scott Hueting; Fabricators: ASI Sign, Davlon Company, Ken Leiberman, Don Asbee; Artists: Courtney Bean, Helena Hernmark, Sheila Hicks.

**Sussman/Prejza &
Company Inc.**

*3960 Ince Blvd.
Culver City, CA 90232
310/836-3939*

*Principals:
Deborah Sussman
Paul Prejza*

*Year Founded: 1968
Size of Firm: 30 plus*

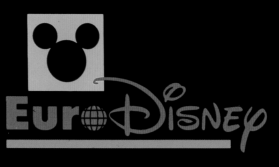

EuroDisney corporate
logo designed for
sponsor use.

Principals and Associates: Seated (l to r): Robert Cordell, Debra Valencia, Scott Cuyler, Deborah Sussman
Standing (l to r): Fernando Vazquez, Mark Nelsen, Paul Prejza.

Directory for
Colorado Place, an
office campus
in Santa Monica.

Freeway-scaled
announcement sign
for Howard Hughes
Center, a 65-acre
mixed-use development.

Key Clients:
Apple Computer,
The Audubon Institute,
Cleveland Cavaliers,
C.J. Segerstrom & Sons,
Disney Development
Company, Esprit
International, Hasbro,
Los Angeles Olympic
Organizing Committee,
Los Angeles
Philharmonic,
Maguire Thomas
Partners, Miyama
Development Company,
Prudential Realty,
The Rouse Company,
Southern California Gas
Company, Times Square
Associates.

Sussman/Prejza & Company Inc.

Two examples of the
international logo
program for LeoPalace
resorts and hotels.

Sussman/Prejza & Company, led
by partners Deborah Sussman and
Paul Prejza, orchestrated, with
the Jerde Partnership, an immensely
popular, intelligent and effective
design program for the 1984 Los Angeles
Olympics. In doing so, they also helped give
environmental graphics a star turn: mainstream
journalism on the '84 Olympics almost never
failed to mention the importance of the
project's design in creating an atmosphere of
festivity and celebration. This success was due
to Sussman/Prejza's ability to coordinate
architecture and graphics so skillfully that it is
difficult to say where one begins and the other
ends. Information and form are seamlessly fused
by a staff that is multi-disciplinary and eager to
blur the professional boundaries between two-
and three-dimensional design. The partners,
with a large staff headed by five associates, have
brought this integrated approach to substantial
projects across the U.S., in Europe and Asia.

Sculptural Assyrian
archers at The Citadel,
a factory outlet center
in the City of Commerce.
The arrows are cables
that support shade
canopies during
the summer months.

Awards platform and
backdrop from the
Swim Venue at the 1984
Summer Olympics.

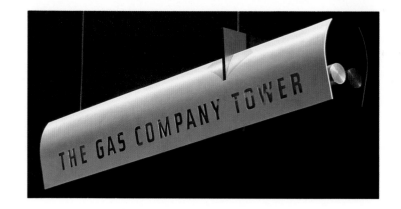

The edge view of the exterior identification sign, fabricated in aluminum, echoes the shape of the new corporate symbol.

Sculptural sconces symbolizing gas flames ring the exterior of The Gas Company Tower in downtown Los Angeles. The sconces were a design alternative to the typical building top identification and were the genesis of a new corporate identity program for The Gas Company, which includes print, vehicle graphics, facility signing and employee uniforms.

The chandelier in the entry lobby enlarges the dimensional flame concept.

The classical layout of The Gas Company stationery system is animated by the flame symbol printed full page on the reverse of the letterhead.

All vehicles in the company's large fleet are identified with the new image and specially designed graphics.

The program for EuroDisney included a system of corporate trademarks and a distinctive palette of colors. This corporate image was also applied to signing, transportation and vehicular graphics. The pedestrian wayfinding system through the hotel district of EuroDisney includes pedestrian directionals, maps, regulatory signs, tram stop identities, and Disney transport signs.

EuroDisney information kiosk with map combines Mickey head icon with French "i" symbolizing information.

Transportation signs identify bus stops and help guide visitors to their destinations.

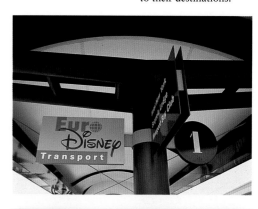

Detail of EuroDisney bus graphics.

The stationery is one of many print applications in a corporate image program that includes annual reports and marketing materials.

Sussman/Prejza & Company Inc.

Chicago was named after the wild onion (che·ca·gou in Illini Indian) which grows along the banks of the river.

Logotype for Chicago Place.

The wild onion symbol was exploded and used as paving patterns on the ground floor. The designs were interpreted in terrazzo in a "prairie" color palette, particular to the Midwest.

Chicago Place, an eight-level retail center, drew from the region's architectural traditions and the wild onion (for which Chicago was named) for its inspirations. In addition to signing, the project involved working closely with Skidmore, Owings & Merrill, the architects, on the building interiors. Sussman/Prejza designed the color, patterning, amenities and details such as the hand railing and elevator cabs.

The symbol for Chicago Place is the wild onion. Its aesthetic is informed by the Prairie Style architecture and designs developed in Chicago in the early part of the century.

An eight-story atrium visually connects the ground floor with the eighth floor garden. An 'Indian headdress' utilizing famous Chicago buildings as 'feathers' provides a focal point for the garden.

Pentagram UK

11 Needham Road
London W11 2RP
(071) 229-3477

Principals, London:
Theo Crosby
Alan Fletcher
Kenneth Grange
David Hillman
Mervyn Kurlansky
John McConnell
David Pocknell
John Rushworth
Peter Saville
Daniel Weil

Year Founded: 1972
Size of Firm:
18 Partners and offices
in London, New York,
San Francisco
Total staff: 140

The Stansted Airport
signage program for the
British Airport Authority
incorporates interior
supergraphic symbols which
can be clearly read at a
distance. Pentagram
designed the location and
information signs with
backlit letters and numerals
set in the chromatic walls.
Partner: Alan Fletcher;
Designers: Alan Fletcher,
Quentin Newark.

The partners from Pentagram's three offices.

For the London
Dockland's Development
Corporation Pentagram
designed large, free-
standing sculptural
arrows made from sheet
steel and coated with
the same paint used on
oil rigs in the North
Sea. The 18-ft., two-ton
arrows have special
fixing points to facilitate
moving them. Partner:
John McConnell;
Designers: John
McConnell, Ralph Selby.

Key Clients:
Arup Associates,
British Airport
Authority,
Co-operative
Retail Services,
Eureka!
The Children's Museum,
London Docklands
Development
Corporation,
Museum of
Modern Art,Oxford;
Tate Gallery,
Victoria and Albert
Museum.

Pentagram UK

Directional signs for
Stockley Park, an
international business park
in London's Green Belt.
The main entrance sign is
a 30-ft. high steel flag with
red aluminum panels
simulating rippling banners.
The flexible aluminum
information panels (below)
can be added or subtracted
on either side as needed.
The lettering is an adapted
form of Firmin Didot.
Partner: David Hillman;
Designers: David Hillman,
Leigh Brownsword.

Pentagram, formed in London in 1972, is an anomaly in the world of design because it eschews the traditional hierarchy of design management and its consequent trickle-down aesthetics. Each of the firm's 18 partners works with their own design team, drawing upon the skills of a staff of 140. This cellular structure is utilized in Pentagram's three offices in New York, San Francisco and London. The unique organization exploits the best of both worlds: the resources of a large-scale firm and the focus and attention to detail of a small firm. It evidently works; Pentagram has produced truly outstanding projects, managing to be at the forefront of intelligent design without succumbing to trends and fads which would become outdated. In the field of environmental graphics, Pentagram has helped define the creative standards and sophistication of this emerging discipline.

Free-standing signs
at the Tate Gallery in
London echo the
columns of the
museum building

Color-coded fabric banners at the entrance to each gallery carry the name of the exhibition in a Bodoni-designed typeface. Each of these are linked to a similarly coded map given to visitors as they come in.

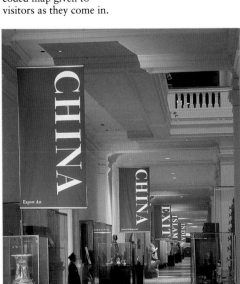

The Victoria and Albert Museum houses Britain's finest collection of applied art and design. The building itself has been added to many times since its opening in 1852. To traffic visitors more efficiently through the museum's complex maze of galleries, Pentagram designed a directional sign system based on a color compass: red for North, green for South, blue for West and yellow for East. Partner: Alan Fletcher; Designers: Alan Fletcher, Quentin Newark; Photographer: Dennis Gilbert.

Pentagram's identity and sign system for The Museum of Modern Art, Oxford, reflects the character of its unusual setting: 20th century art in a converted 19th century brewery. The building's architectural layout of grids and cast iron columns inspired the linear pattern of the directional signage, while the bold sans serif lettering provided a strong contemporary look. Partner: Mervyn Kurlansky; Designers: Mervyn Kurlansky, Robert Dunnet.

The information panel is a scrolled sheet of black enamel painted steel. Clear letters of sans serif type are white on a black background.

In developing an updated identity
and sign system for Leo's co-operative
foodstore chain, Pentagram created
a strong graphic foundation based on a
simple use of red, black and white.
The entrance sign is a white cube erected
above the store. The sign carries the
store's Bodoni-based logotype which has
360-degrees visibility. Prominent red
diamonds that echo the logotype were
used throughout the interior to identify
the traditional aisles and check-out
areas. Woodcut illustrations identify
different food and item areas. Partner:
Mervyn Kurlansky; Designers:
Mervyn Kurlansky, Robert Dunnet.

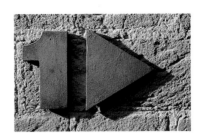

Secondary information is presented using black and grey decals that are inexpensive and simple to change.

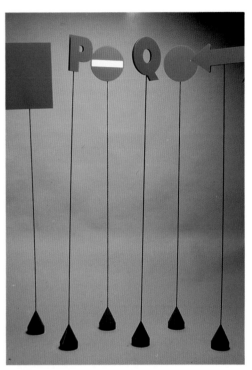

For the Tate Gallery in Liverpool, Pentagram designed a sign system in keeping with the building's original features. The main floor signs were produced in cast iron and positioned flush to the walls. A series of mobile temporary signs, made of brightly painted aluminum mounted on tall steel rods attached to weighted bases, were developed to indicate gallery closures, queueing points and directions to events. Partner: David Hillman; Designers: David Hillman, Jo Swindell.

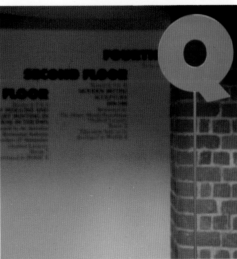

Signs for Broadgate financial services development were produced in two versions: free-standing solid bronze units and wall-mounted sheet brass fixtures. These were chemically treated to produce a black patina on the surfaces. Directional information was engraved and highlighted with white paint. Partner: John McConnell; Designers: John McConnell, David Lum.

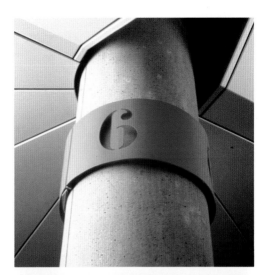

A solid granite marker acts as a crash barrier to protect the building. Etched with the address and a decorative compass evoking Lloyd's nautical past, the cornerstone functions on a more practical level as seating.

Laser-cut aluminum panels are applied to walls and interior spaces. Below, a men's restroom sign.

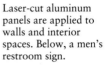

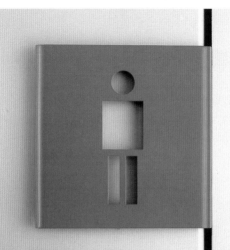

The sign program for the new headquarters of Lloyd's of London complements the building's innovative architecture by Richard Rogers. Using a precision-engineered stencil alphabet by Le Corbusier, each letter and number was laser cut out of aluminum panels and then stove-enamelled in primary colors. Partner: Alan Fletcher; Designers: Alan Fletcher, Nick Simmons.

By Alan Fletcher

The 1949 Protocol

The cliché, French for "printing block", is a graphic means of repetition ad infinitum.

Clichés survive long after the conditions that produced them are dead. In language we go on about "pigs in pokes," "leading horses to water,"and being "dogs in mangers." Although banal, the cliché is readily understood by everybody–something Sam Goldwyn appreciated when, on hearing a complaint that a script was full of them, promptly told his director to introduce some more. The most common (and oldest) visual cliché is the pointing finger. For some reason, to point is considered vulgar. The American film director John Ford used to say it was only socially permissible to point at pimps, pastries and producers. He probably had Sam Goldwyn in mind: In Hollywood the cliché of a producer is an obese, cigar-chomping philistine who is bent on sacrificing art to the lowest common denominator of the market. Anyway, the second oldest visual cliché has to be the arrow. Once when driving from Rome to Brescia, Jean-Michel Folon reckoned he counted over a thousand different kinds of directional arrow. A small sampling, but nevertheless a clear indication that when the need is to provoke a response rather than a thought, the cliché is essential. Furthermore, they are generally better than anything one can think of to replace them.

International road signs date from the 1949 Protocol, the result of a convention held in Geneva in that year. No one remembers who designed them, but judging from results it must have been a committee. Anyway, despite their crudity, the pictorial versions function reasonably well. I once attended a lecture by a Polish designer who showed photographs taken around the world of two little people holding hands inside a red triangle. None were the same, yet each was instantly recognizable. The more ambiguous pictograms are less happy as although most people understand the significance of the man putting up a large umbrella, the sign that implies "Beware of low-flying motorcycles" really means something else. Then there are the abstracts, which have no link before form and meaning–either you know them or you don't. Apparently many don't. A recent survey unnervingly revealed that only seven percent of drivers realize a white circle with a red rim means "No Vehicles."

Anyway, what really separates the designer sheep from the designer goats is the ability to stroke a cliché until it purrs like a metaphor.

Alan Fletcher trained at the Royal College of Art in London and the School of Architecture and Design at Yale University. He co-founded Fletcher/ Forbes/Gill in 1959 and since 1972 was a partner and and co-founder of Pentagram, whose clients include IBM Europe, Lloyd's of London, and Scandinavian Airlines, among many others. Internationally recognized for his work, Fletcher has lectured and served on design juries throughout the U.S. and Europe. In 1982 the Society of Industrial Artists and Designers awarded him their annual Medal for outstanding achievement in design.

A cliché everyone understands. A selection of graphic "pointing finger" directional pictograms from the personal collection of Alan Fletcher.

**Whitehouse &
Company**

18 East 16th Street
New York, New York
10003
212/206-1080

Principal:
Roger Whitehouse

Year Founded: 1978
Size of Firm: 12

A director of the Society
for Environmental
Graphic Design, Roger
Whitehouse was the lead
author of the SEGD
White Paper, which
represented the
professional response
to and interpretation of
the Americans with
Disabilities Act (ADA).

Principal of Whitehouse and Company, Roger Whitehouse RIBA.

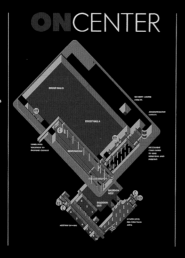

The main exhibition
halls of the Onondoga
County Convention
Center are identified by
letters rotated out of
swirl-finished aluminum
planes. A naming and
identity program
resulted in the ONcenter
logotype, as a more
accessible interpretation
of the full formal name.

Comprehensive
wayfinding and signage
program and graphic
standards manual

Key Clients:
Coudert Brothers
Attorneys,
Dewey Ballantine
Attorneys,
Gwathmey Siegel
Architects,
Herman Miller, The
High Museum, IBM,
Knoll International,
Lincoln Center for
the Performing Arts,
Metropolitan Museum
of Art, M.I.T.,
Mitchell/Giurgola
Architects,
People's Bank,
Pratt Institute,
Princeton University,
Sotheby's,
Richard Meier &
Partners Architects,
The Prudential,
Virginia Air
& Space Center,
Edward Larrabee
Barnes/M.Y. Lee
Architects.

Whitehouse & Company

Porcelain enamel plaque
celebrating the opening
of Richard Meier's
High Museum of Art
in Atlanta.

Catalog covers on
movable stanchions act
as wayfinding icons to
identify exhibits or
auctions at Sotheby's
New York headquarters.
Other movable
components allow for
instant updating of
information.

Roger Whitehouse has a unique perspective on environmental graphics that emerges from his original training as an architect. His sensibility spans both the architectural concerns of planning and analysis and the typographic and pictorial concerns of graphic design. The result is a studio centered on information-driven design, with a predilection for elegant typography. This focus has lead Whitehouse & Company into multi-disciplinary projects that combine signage, print, video, and multimedia. Whitehouse has taken an active role in shaping the field of environmental graphics through his involvement with the Society for Environmental Graphic Design. He has been a particularly effective advocate for universal design for individuals with disabilities, helping to draft standards for signage that serve the widest possible range of audiences. This philosophy, driven equally by architectural context and informational clarity, have brought the studio into frequent collaboration with public and institutional clients, ranging from museums and performing arts centers to health care complexes and universities.

Whitehouse & Company
has designed interactive
animated multimedia
projects to document the
Graphic Standards for
Pratt Institute; as an
explanation of the
geometry of the Golden
Mean for an exhibit at
the AIA Convention in
1993; and for product
introduction for Project
Furniture in the U.K.

Dramatic images from
the NASA collection,
designed to be
reproduced in full color
on porcelain enamel
panels, are to remind
motorists of the level
on which they are
parked in the Space
Center's garage.

*When NASA decided to relocate their
main Visitor Center from Langley to
Hampton, Virginia, Roger Whitehouse
proposed using one of their most
dramatic pieces of hardware, the
Manned Maneuvering Unit (MMU),
as the basic component of the graphic
identity program and the major
identifying element of the building.
Secondary signs, such as those
for bathrooms, transform the internationally recognized symbols
for Men and Women into members
of the Space Program.*

At night, the identifying MMU is designed to stand out against the entire museum display which is revealed through a massive glass wall beneath the soaring roof structure of architects Mitchell/Giurgola's dramatic new building.

In 1990, Roger Whitehouse set out to design the 'ultimate' sign system, which would combine all the benefits of 'off-the-shelf' modularity and repeatability with the complete flexibility of custom systems. Originally designed for Knoll International, the patented 'Infinity' system is now marketed worldwide by ASI Sign Systems and A/S Modulex and is being used as the basis of sign programs by many internationally renowned designers.

These plaques are part of a series designed by Roger Whitehouse to demonstrate the esthetic and functional flexibility of the system.

A custom computer design and ordering program, created specifically for the Infinity System by Bob Cox and Luis Pineiros, allows users to 'build' a sign system in full color on screen, while at the same time estimating cost of unit, and generating contract drawings and schedules.

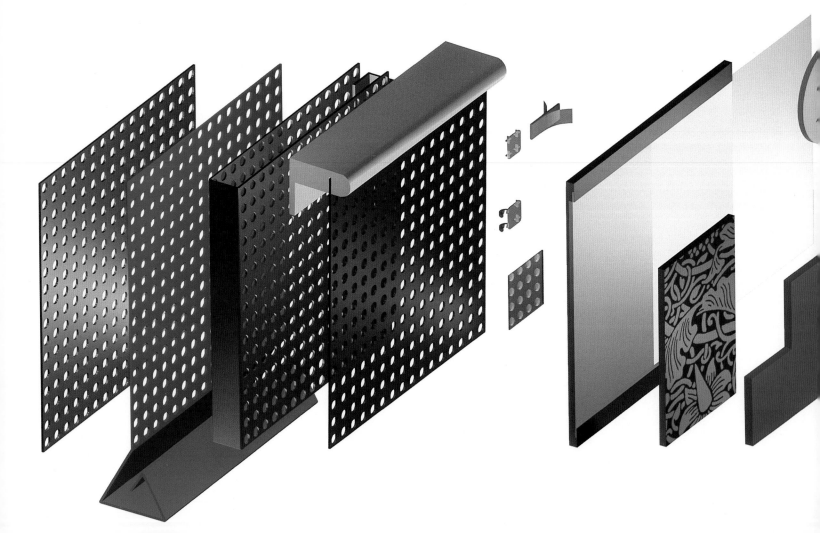

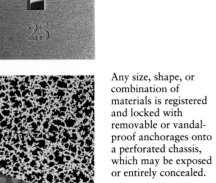

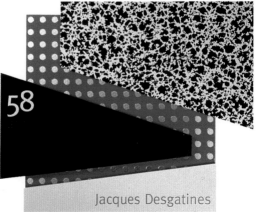

Any size, shape, or combination of materials is registered and locked with removable or vandal-proof anchorages onto a perforated chassis, which may be exposed or entirely concealed.

A system of plug-in 'pips' can be used to create custom arrows, icons or pictograms.

Not only are all graphics generated from electronic masters, but shapes of any complexity are laser or water-jet cut from computer templates. Both processes ensure complete accuracy when reordering components to maintain the system.

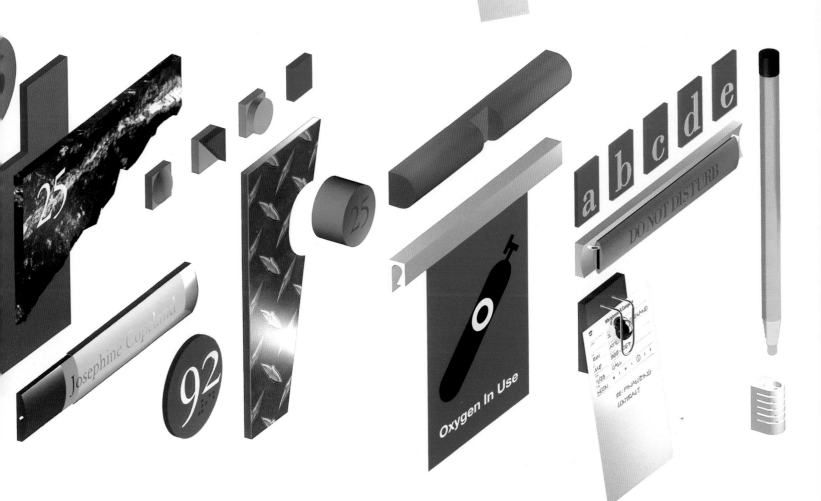

*The new identity program for Pratt
Institute in New York, one of America's
foremost design schools, exemplifies
the versatility made possible by building
on a strong conceptual foundation.
The basic mark is a bold and assertive
statement, consonant with the school's
location and self-proclaimed image.
Flexibility and the ability to modify
the mark are key components of
the program. For example, the addition
of punctuation reinforces the school's
role in communications.*

Pratt... Pratt? Pratt!

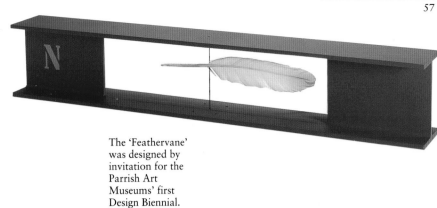

The 'Feathervane' was designed by invitation for the Parrish Art Museums' first Design Biennial.

The conceptual basis for the identity of Richard Meier's renovated Barnum Museum was an 'acrobatic B' which reflected both Barnum's showmanship and the sophistication of the new museum.

Graphics for Hartford Seminary extend the architectural language of Richard Meier's landmark building into the sign system.

Designers who worked with Roger Whitehouse on these projects are: Peter Katz-HMA plaque and Hartford Seminary; Mary Elliott-Virginia Air & Space Center and HUP; Jamie Jett and Kanchen Rajanna-Harmony by Design; Jonathan Posnett-Pratt and Infinity. The Pratt Institute identity program was designed as part of a collaborative team including Cheryl Lewin and Pratt faculty members Moira Cullen, D.K. Holland, and Christian Simms. The Harmony by Design and Project FX

multimedia presentations were completed in collaboration with Beverly Russell. Co-authors with Roger Whitehouse on the ADA White Paper were Ken Ethridge AIA and Nora Olgyay. The diagram for 'Infinity' was modeled and rendered by Michael Crumpton of MicroColor Inc., NYC. The photographer for Pratt was Scott Francis; for Infinity, Scott Francis, Kelly Campbell and Bart Lee. 'Infinity' is a registered trademark of ASI Sign Systems Inc.

**Walt Disney
Imagineering**

*1401 Flower Street
Glendale, CA 91221
818/544-6500*

Year Founded: 1952

*Size of Graphic Design
Department: 30*

A planter stanchion at World Bazaar, Tokyo Disneyland directs parents to lost children and the Baby Center. It is made from fiberglass reinforced polyester to resemble wood and metal.

At Adventureland in Tokyo Disneyland, a food cart graphic incorporates boldly colored typography silkscreened on metal, evocative of turn-of-the-century typefaces.

Color comps of signs for Clock Repair marquee and 101st Engine Company window graphic for Mickey's Toontown, Disneyland. Comps are made from colored marker on board.

Walt Disney Imagineering

Cast acrylic sculpture
is the focal point of
the entrance marquee
to EPCOT Center,
Walt Disney World.

Walt Disney Imagineering was founded in 1952, when Walt Disney assembled a group of artists, writers, technicians, and craftsmen to create Disneyland Park. Graphic Design, just one of Imagineering's 150 disciplines, is responsible for all Disney Theme Park signage, from the grand marquees that draw guests into spectacular adventures to the operational graphics identifying restrooms and telephones. Whether the language is English, Japanese, or French, environmental signs are friendly, helpful inhabitants of the Disney Theme Parks. For Euro Disneyland in France, the Graphic Design department created 4,455 signs in over a dozen styles, including Victorian (Main Street, USA), American Southwestern (Frontierland), African, Middle Eastern, and Caribbean (Adventureland), French, English, German, and Italian (Fantasyland), and Art Deco, Industrial, and Science Fiction (Discoveryland). The latest of Imagineering's Graphic Design projects is a family of zany, humorous graphics for Mickey's Toontown at Disneyland– including several automated signs that seem to have a life of their own.

Walt Disney World logo
design is applied as a
Magic Kingdom train's
sand dome graphic,
screen printed on brass.

A sense of surprise and whimsy are primary elements in many of the sign projects at Disney, whether applied to parking lot identification or restaurant marquees. Typography, bright colors and engaging characters help keep visitors aware of where they are at any point in their travels, as well as invite them to refreshments or guide them to facilities.

Sid Cahuenga's One-of-a-Kind, vehicle graphic hand-painted on metal; Hollywood Blvd., Disney-MGM Studios, Walt Disney World.

The Endor Vendors shop marquee entrance sign is fabricated from found objects, leather and aluminum; Backlot Annex, Disney-MGM Studios, Walt Disney World.

Donald Duck demonstrates his lasso abilities in this Western 41-44 parking lot aisle identification made of aluminum, steel and porcelain enamel; Disney-MGM Studios, Walt Disney World.

Sci-Fi Dine-In Theater Restaurant marquee is made of aluminum, cast fiberglass and neon; Backlot Annex, Disney-MGM Studios, Walt Disney World.

A foam study model
for Gadget's Go Coaster
marquee in Mickey's
Toontown, Disneyland.

Cast iron street sign at
crossing of Pirate Al
and D'Orleans in
New Orleans Square,
Disneyland.

The Mad Hatter's mad
hat greets shoppers at
Main Street, U.S.A.
in Disneyland. The shop
marquee is made of
aluminum metal.

Marche aux Fleurs/Sacs
et Modes, fashionable
accessories shop in
Disneyland's New
Orleans Square, has a
bracketed shop marquee
made from bronze
and art glass. The
marquee measures 38
by 33 inches.

Intricate detailing and attention to historical references are hallmarks of the graphic design and signage projects throughout many of the special Disney environments. Since many of the attractions are reproductions of entire city districts, such as New Orleans Square, signage projects incorporate authentic design elements from the period.

At New Orleans Square in Disneyland, identification signs at Cristal d'Orleans shop and Club 33 Restaurant are intricately cut in glue chip mirror and bronze.

The Bengal Barbecue restaurant marquee, at Adventureland, is made of cast fiberglass and reinforced polyester to resemble carved wood and polished rock.

Adventure Isle map
exterior sign board is
painted aluminum panel
on wood; Adventureland,
Euro Disneyland.

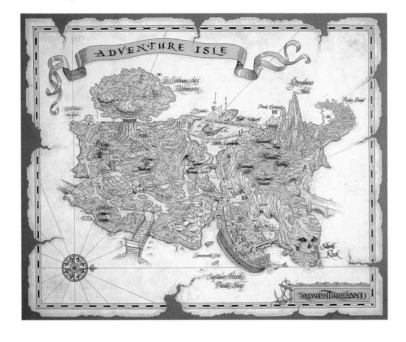

Color comp of Phantom
Manor marquee in
Frontierland at Euro
Disneyland.

*For Euro Disneyland, the newest
Disney Theme Park, the Walt Disney
Imagineering Graphic Design
Department generated 4,455 signs in
a diversity of international styles,
including French, English, German,
Italian, Middle Eastern and African.
Each of the Euro Disneyland themed
lands is a perfect extension of its
graphic environment. Every detail is
perfectly designed to complement
each attraction's decorative theme.*

Cast brass railing
medallion for Euro
Disneyland Railroad in
Main Street, U.S.A.

The wall-mounted shop marquee of Constellations, at Euro Disneyland's Discoveryland, is made of cast bronze, glass and neon.

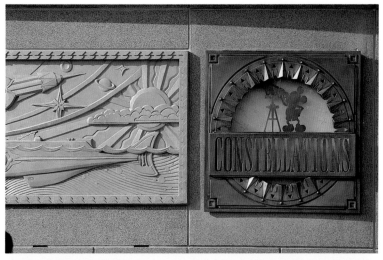

Poster of Adventure Isle and the Euro Disney Railroad are serigraphs printed on Tyvek; Euro Disneyland.

At Euro Disneyland's Discoveryland, the marquee entrance to Le Visionarium, is a free-standing rotating sphere fabricated from polished brass, bronze and copper on a granite base.

838 Broadway, 6th Floor
New York, NY 10003
212/674-0280

Principal:
Keith Godard

Year Founded: 1968
Size of Firm: 5

Detail of a drawing from
one of the relief sketches
for the plaques.

Keith Godard, principal of StudioWorks.

*I would like to thank
the following designers
and people that have
over the years helped
me realize the work
in this book.
Partners: Lester Walker,
Craig Hodgetts,
Robert Mangurian,
Peter de Bretteville,
Stephanie Tevonian,
Hans van Dijk;*

*Designers, Assistants
and Writers: Christy
Trotter, Jamie Jett,
Kim Powick, Marnie
Krooss, Mark Donnolo,
Jennifer Schuman,
Janet Giampietro,
Rose Kowalski, Jeri
Froehlich, Jennifer
Tobias, Herb Rosenthal,
Peter Green, Debbie
Nevins, Rebecca
Shanor, Robert Dye,
Robert Kahn, Elizabeth
Blades, Yoko Satomi,
Garry Faro, Wayne
Walker, Jim Mellor,
Laurie Beckelman,
Olga Lavie, Toby
Bottorf, Kate Hixon,
Bill Gold, Andy
Ackerman, Charles
Platt, Steve Bono,
Benno Wissing, and
Katrin Adam.*

*Five of a series of 14 commemorative
plaques designed for the celebration of
the Brooklyn Bridge Centennial. The
plaques show how the Bridge was built,
which was completed in 1883, and
New York harbor as it appeared at that
time. To make a comparison, the older
buildings are in relief and those built in
1983 are in intaglio. Each text was acid
etched in silicone bronze and the bas
reliefs were cast in french sand. They are
installed on the railings around the
towers and overlook the vistas from the
Bridge. Fabricator: Excalibur Bronze;
Sculptor: Domenico Facci.*

Key Clients:
Brooklyn Bridge
Centennial Commission,
New York City
Department
of Transportation,
Staten Island
Children's Museum,
Lincoln Center,
Cornell University,
P.T. Barnum
Museum/People's Bank,
New York Landmarks
Conservancy,
J. Paul Getty Museum,
Children's Museum
of Manhattan,
Harvard Business
School Press,
United Nations,
New York City
Department of
Economic Development,
New York
Hall of Science,
Creative Discovery
Museum, Chattanooga.

Keith Godard/ StudioWorks

StudioWorks, which originated as Works in 1968, has brought humor, theater, and ingenuity to the design of exhibitions, signage, and publications. Keith Godard, the studio principal, probes the boundaries between fact and fiction, the real and the surreal. His exhibitions on aspects of New York's history–such as the building of the Brooklyn Bridge–are researched with scholarly rigor and executed with playful wit. Born in England, educated at Yale, Godard has focused on design that reaches diverse audiences. Perhaps the toughest of these is children. One of Godard's brilliant projects was the exhibition "Look and Look Again: Children's Art from Armenia" at the Children's Museum of Manhattan. In this project, photographs of the Armenian landscape were embedded in the gallery's wall, visible through holes pierced at child's-eye-level. Thus the children's artwork was exhibited on walls that thematized the distance between Manhattan and Yeravan.

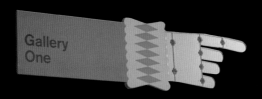

The signage for the Staten Island Children's Museum at Snug Harbor, New York incorporates the gestures of sign language in a whimsical way, which gives visual stimulation as well as communicate direction. The materials used were the same as in the work for the Lincoln Center project, along with chalkboards which reinforced the concept of participation. Fabricators: Gary Faro/Wayne Walker.

**Keith Godard/
StudioWorks**

A simple tug-'o-war
and basic principle
of a clothes line display,
illustrates how a
suspension bridge
is constructed.

Within the vaults,
the Bridge's cables and
anchor plates are
concealed. Orange neon
describes their position
and actual size.

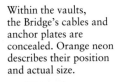

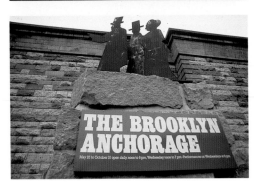

*For the Brooklyn Bridge Centennial
celebration, an opening exhibition called
"The Anatomy of the Brooklyn Bridge,"
was installed in the huge vaults of the
bridge's Brooklyn Anchorage. Illustrating
the stages of the Bridge's construction,
the exhibition enabled visitors to view
the project in the vast space amidst
traffic sounds overhead, giving them a
vivid idea of the complexity of building
the Brooklyn Bridge. At the entrance,
a Cor-ten steel sculpture of John,
Washington and Emily Roebling, the
bridge's designers, greets visitors.*

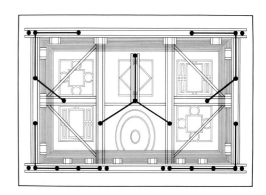

Exhibition plan and floor graphics are representative of the actual travertine floor inside the Customs House.

Directional signs in the Lincoln Center theatre corridors incorporate brightly colored formica and blackboards (for shadows) to create a trompe l'oeil spot light effect. The red 'spot lights' guided actors to the rehearsal rooms and the green ones to the ballet rooms. Yellow 'spots' helped find the way back. Fabricator: Sign Here Now, Inc.

"The Palace of Commerce," was an outdoor pavilion installed at the U. S. Customs House, at Bowling Green in Lower Manhattan. Positioned in front of the building's granite Beaux Arts facade, the pavilion is a bright, optimistic feature. The exhibition traces the development of the area as a site of finance and trade in the city's history, describes the architectural competition for the building (won by Cass Gilbert), and illustrates the importance of its preservation and use as a cultural facility. Text: Deborah Nevins; Construction: Gary Faro/Wayne Walker.

Model of exhibit.

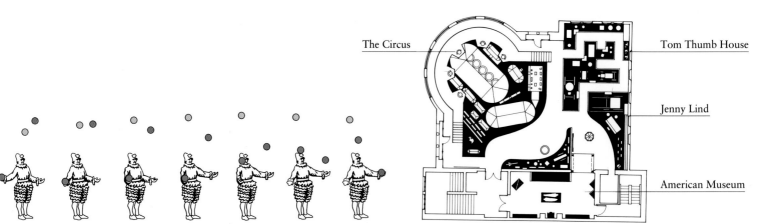

The Circus

Tom Thumb House

Jenny Lind

American Museum

The designer's sensitivity to the individual subjects is given a good example in the Tom Thumb display (far left), in which artifacts are raised up in a "glass house configuration" and viewed as if the visitor were 36 inches tall. Visitors are given a big "Welcome" to the entrance of the Jenny Lind exhibition area.

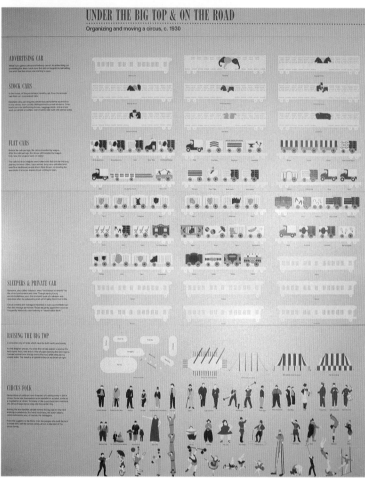

The exhibition design for the P.T. Barnum Museum in Bridgeport, Connecticut has the spirit of Barnum, but with a contemporary appeal. Original artifacts were integrated with fabricated exhibits and anecdotal texts. A mini environment within the overall exhibit (see plan), the various subjects and spaces tell the story of Barnum's American Museum, his times and travels with Jenny Lind, his admiration and entrepreneurship with Tom Thumb and at age 65, his management of the Circus. The overall view of the museum displays the working model of the Circus, made by Bill Brinley, and the "Barnum in the Clouds" feature, a video display of the Barnum Circus with animated posters. Clients: City of Bridgeport and People's Bank; Exhibition Director: Katzalyst; Fabricator: Rathe Productions; Interior Renovation Architect: Richard Meier & Partners.

Tickets for Nevsky gala.
Characters from the film
are representative of the
evenings' various events.

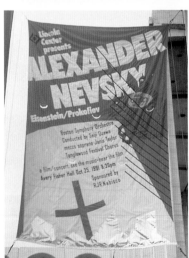

A selection of banners designed for
"Live from Lincoln Center" and the
gala benefit evening of the premiere
of Alexander Nevsky, Eisenstein's 1938
film with orchestra and chorus. Each
of the Center's three main buildings,
The New York State Theater,
The Metropolitan Opera House, and
Avery Fisher Hall have banners
displaying separate musical and
theatrical events.

5th Floor	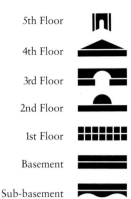
4th Floor	
3rd Floor	
2nd Floor	
1st Floor	
Basement	
Sub-basement	

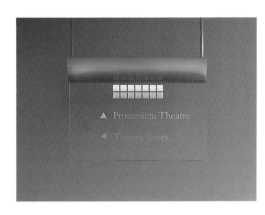

Hanging sign of sandblasted plate glass with lettering and floor icon that is edge-lit from a light source above.

Exterior view of the Center, showing banners. Photographer: ©Richard Bryant.

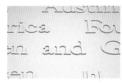

Detail of relief letters.

Over 100 donors' names are displayed along the loggia wall at the Center's entrance.

Donor recognition and directional signage program for Cornell University Center for the Performing Arts, Ithaca, New York. Throughout a variety of spaces inside and outside the Center, donors' names are inscribed on relief letter friezes that have painted edges lit from above by cold-cathode neon. To orient visitors around the building, a floor-level icon (see above) was designed and adapted from architectural representations of the building's exterior features. Because of the site's complex levels, symbols help in wayfinding. Architect: James Stirling/ Michael Wilford, London.

Wayne Hunt Design

87 North Raymond
Avenue, #215
Pasadena, CA 91103
818/793-7847

Principal:
Wayne Hunt

Year Founded: 1977
Size of Firm: 7

Responding to the
Architect's request for
extreme understatement,
Wayne Hunt Design
created signs for
California Plaza in Los
Angeles that used letters
incised and etched into
metal and glass surfaces.
With Don Clark Design;
Architect: Arthur
Erikson Associates.

Wayne Hunt, principal of Wayne Hunt Design.

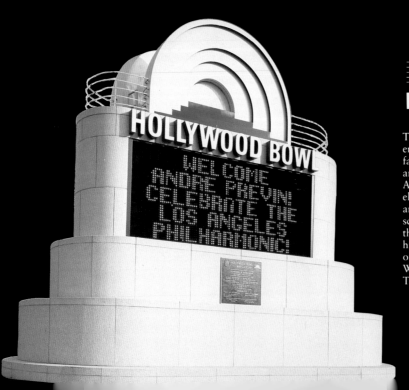

The marquee to the
entrance of the world
famous Hollywood Bowl
amphitheater in Los
Angeles features an
electronic message board
and neon-enhanced
sculptural application of
the logo. The two-storey
high structure is made
of granite. Designer:
Wayne Hunt; Architect:
Tanzmann Associates.

Key Clients:
City of Culver City,
City of Pasadena,
County of
Los Angeles,
Knott's Berry Farm,
MCA Recreation
Services,
Melvin Simon,
Simpson Paper,
Unocal Corporation,
Walt Disney Company.

Colorful graphics and
abstract interpretations
of time dominate
these clocks designed
to Novita.

Wayne Hunt's signage programs, with their populist aesthetic, respond directly to their settings: in huge malls, his design manages to speak as loudly as any other sign; in bland public buildings, this same aesthetic serves to inflect the environment with humor and color. The firm's work is exuberant in its exaggeration of scale, color and typography: a sign for the Wilderness Theatre constructs type out of timbers: it is "vernacular" without a trace of condescension. Other projects evidence a conceptual approach to signage: for the Children's Court of Los Angeles County, self-portraits by children in the dependency court system are a graphic reminder to visitors of the real lives which pass through an otherwise anonymous building.

The signing program for
The Port of Long Beach
consists of over 100
large roadside signing
elements. As part of a
site communication
enhancement process
prior to the design,
Wayne Hunt Design
helped rename many
port streets and
renumber the piers.

Use of alphabetical and
numeric elements are
designed to enable
commuters to easily read
and understand road
directions while driving.
Designers: Wayne Hunt,
Sharrie Lee, John
Temple; Architect:
Morris/Deasy Partners.

In designing the sign program for the Edmund C. Edelman Children's Court for the County of Los Angeles, Wayne Hunt Design concentrated on creating a space where children would feel comfortable and unthreatened. This unique building is the first court dedicated to children's issues. All of the graphics, and the building itself, were designed to child and family guidelines. Wherever possible, non-verbal systems were used. Other design elements incorporated boldly painted signage for facilities and floor direction guides. Each floor features a pictorial image (house, star, moon, etc.)as an organizing device. Designers: Wayne Hunt, John Temple, Sharrie Lee and Katherine Go; Architect: Kajima Associates.

The entrance to The Children's Court is a bright, open geometric design which reiterates the logo and reinforces the feeling of being in a house. A graphic field of self portraits painted by children were used as a welcoming, familiar theme. The portraits were enlarged onto porcelain enamel panels for permanent display.

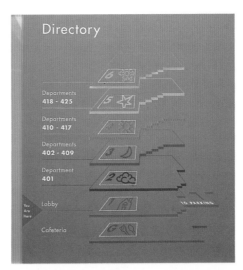

Wall directories are clearly marked with individual floor locations and department offices for that floor. Throughout the system, whimsical steel sculptures of suns and half moons atop brightly painted pedestals catch attention.

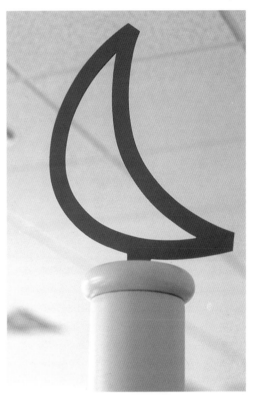

Brightly colored pictographs help organize the wayfinding system throughout the building.

The signage for the Wilderness Theater was created to simulate an Old West effect using lettering made out of wooden logs. Schematic rendering at right of the Ripsaw structure gives an overview of the use of these Western architectural design elements.

Signage for Snoopy's boutique and Mrs. Knott's Restaurant use cartoon illustrations of both characters.

Inside the world's largest shopping mall, The Mall of America, is Knott's Camp Snoopy, the world's largest indoor theme park. Wayne Hunt Designed created a sign system themed to the attractions of the park's famous cartoon characters and the Knott's Berry Farm food products. Throughout the system, Snoopy and Friends appear on wall signs and directional banners which combine large graphic lettering with three-dimensional sculptural elements. Designers: Wayne Hunt, Sharrie Lee, John Temple, Katherine Go; Additional Design: Robin Hall and Tracey Caviola of Knott's.

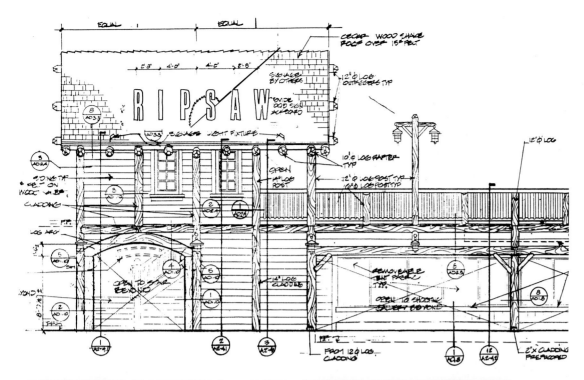

Preliminary sketch and finished sign for Mrs. Knott's Picnic Basket use bold illustration and color to create an animated, graphic display.

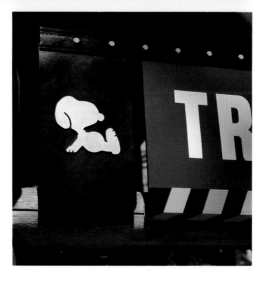

Snoopy's familiar silhouette decorates a mock mud flap in a parody of big rig trucks.

Large cutout fantasy
figures enhance the
Conpac furniture trade
show in California.
Designers: Wayne Hunt,
Katherine Go.

For the Bill of Rights Bicentennial Exhibit for Unocal Corporation, Wayne Hunt Design created free-standing displays illustrating each of the basic rights and amendments described in the Bill. Enamel painted red, white and blue stars and stripes at the base of each column are weighted for stability. Designers: Wayne Hunt, John Temple, Sharrie Lee, Katherine Go; Fabricator: Richards Sedor, Temple City, California.

Old Pasadena signs use the historic architectural shape as a graphic element in the logo and sign frames.

The sign program for The City of Pasadena's Old Pasadena project was created as part of the revitalization of the city's historic district. The program consists of off-site directional signs, entrance gateways and in-area directional and identification signs. Designers: Wayne Hunt, Brian Deputy.

Bureau Mijksenaar

Dreeftoren
Haaksbergweg 15
1101 BP
Amsterdam Bullewijk
+31 20 691 47 29
Fax: +31 20 691 72 69

Principal:
Paul Mijksenaar

Year Founded: 1986
Size of Firm: 9

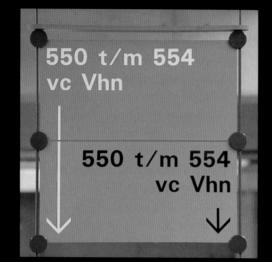

Signs for PTT Post
Distribution centers.
Each pendular sign
corresponds with a
specific mail container.

Clockwise, from left to right: Jurriaan Grolman, Rijk Boerma, Paul Mijksenaar,
Elise de Jong, Martijn Geerdes, Henk van Alst, Ellen de Ringh de Vries,
Ingrid Ho, Annemarie van den Bos. In the background are the office Bureau
Mijksenaar. Photographer: Joost Guntenaar.

Bureau Mijksenaar

Amsterdam Municipal
Transport, GVB,
Dutch Railway Museum,
Graficus Magazine,
Passage Shopping Mall,
PTT Post,
PTT Telecom,
Royal PTT Nederland,
Schiphol
Amsterdam Airport,
Spruijt Printers,
Videotex Nederland,
Zuiderzee Museum.

Bureau Mijksenaar emphasizes the functional aspects of design by applying the insights of ergonomic research and analyzing the way users interact with environmental graphics. Their analytical approach and theoretical orientation sets them apart from their peers in the Netherlands. For Mijksenaar, every aspect of environmental graphics – traffic flow, marketing, software – is subject to, and contingent upon, effective design. Sign systems, maps, and exhibitions are the most important "final product." Bureau Mijksenaar is aware that space, in and out of doors, is limited in installing more and more signs. The answer should be found in designing environmental attributes which can "speak for themselves."

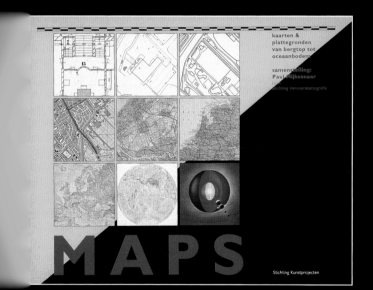

Cover and spread of a travelling exhibition about maps, based on material from the collection of Foundation Archive Paul Mijksenaar.

During a course at Delft University of Technology, Paul Mijksenaar showed how London Transport's famous Underground map could be improved by adding topographical information.

White type on blue is used on primary information signs directed to automobile drivers, and secondary information is in black type on yellow.

Primary and secondary destinations is distinguished by the use of color, which communicates important information to passengers quickly.

Signs and flight information system for Amsterdam Schipol Airport. Expansion at Schiphol Airport includes a new Terminal wing, a fifth concourse, an additional covered parking garage and an elevated road system. For this long-term project, Bureau Mijksenaar is a consultant for all public information media, from maps and flight information to signage. Photographer: Fridtjof Versnel.

A new family of pictographs, based closely on the international standardized symbols, were designed for the airport. Some of the designs were improved, such as 'Transfer', 'Way Out', 'Rent-a-Telephone Center', and 'Europe Custom Cleared Baggage'.

A secondary sign. White typefaces are used for dark-colored signs and black is used for light-colored signs.

A dynamic array of more than 20 different layouts are designed to display various types of flight information on 1600 color television screens.

The unique display has a consistent use of color scheme, layout, and the use of a Frutiger typeface on each screen.

uit from		vlucht flight	
Wenen	IE	714	
Vancouver	NX	330	
enen Zurich	KL	333	
Zurich	SR	14	
ussel vertraag(	BMA	3405	
Tener via Mala(	SPL	2001	
Ouagadougou	NN	241	

KLM · swissair · AIR MALTA · KLM

Vluchten Flights

tijd time	bestemming destination	vlucht flight		gate gate	bijzonderheden remarks
13:45	Frankfurt Munich Zurich Vienna	2001	SA 2	D8	instappen
14:15	Malta	MCK	622	C12	alle klassen
14:55	Eindhoven Brussels	KL	3401	F2	royal class
15:05	Dublin	IE	714	E3	

Vertrekkende vlucht Departing flight

swissair

tijd time	bestemming destination	vlucht flight		bijzonderheden remarks
10:55	Brussels Zurich	SA	622	vertraagd tot 11:05

Volgende vlucht Next flight

13:45	Frankfurt Munich	BMA	3401

Let op! gatewijziging Attention! gate change

09:35	iami Lon	KL	674	gatewijziging	G6
09:35	)s Angeles Bos|	BA	823	gatewijziging	C16

	P1	Aankomst Arrivals
↑		Wegbrengen Passenger escort
		Basistarief f 3,- per uur Initial charge per hour
←	P3	Lang parkeren Long term parking
		Basistarief f 40,- voor 5 dagen Initial charge for 5 days
←	P9	Passagiers Passengers
		Basistarief f 3,- per uur Initial charge per hour

Information regarding parking tariffs at various parking lots. Each group of destinations representing the same direction is indicated by a rounded bar and arrow.

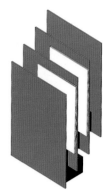

Telephones can be purchased or subscribed at a wide range of stores in Holland. The PTT Telecom desk is easily recognizable by signage and folder-racks.

A wide variety of signs, based on corporate design, help direct visitors to PTT offices.

Sign programs for the Royal PTT Nederland (KPN), the Dutch PTT Post and PTT Telecom Company. The program includes route maps and fire-escape instructions. Special attention is paid to creating clear instructions for manufacturers. A proposal for a 19-storey high meta-sign was not executed; the name 'PTT' was formed using mirrorlike glazing panels, as were used in other parts of the facade.

In the sign system for the Amsterdam Tourist Office, large freestanding maps are used as a key to a network of pedestrian routes to places of interest. The typeface, designed in 1948 by Van Krimpen a.o., is identical to the standardized street signs in Amsterdam.

Sign system for the Amsterdam Metro, created during a partnership with the Werkgroep Bewegwijzering Metro Amersterdam; Peter Brattinga, chairman.

The Zuiderzeemuseum in Enkhuizen can only be reached by ferry; a non-verbal diagram shows the routes of each vessel.

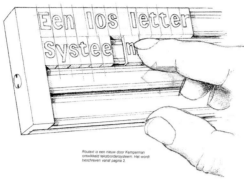

Green signs indicate directions to other reception areas that are coded by single alphabet letters. Below are directional signs for reception areas D/E/F and G/H.

Instructions and example of 'Routext,' a modular sign system designed for Kemperman, Amsterdam. It was used, along with other systems, for the majority of the PTT buildings in Holland.

Instead of using a huge amount of confusing medical terminology, the sign system developed for Total Design, Amsterdam for Amsterdam's VU-Ziekenhuis Hospital simplifies access to the different department areas by using a single character code for each location. Blue areas indicate "Here Is" information and green areas indicate "There Is". Above, signs indicate that you are at 'Begane grond' (ground floor) or at 'Reception M', where you can be directed to other specific medical departments (A-Z).

Entrance sign for the
Sporthallen Zuid,
a municipal sports center
in Amsterdam. Sixteen
mirrors (normally used
at dangerous curves
or exits at rural roads)
reflect the buildings which
otherwise cannot be seen
from this vantage point.

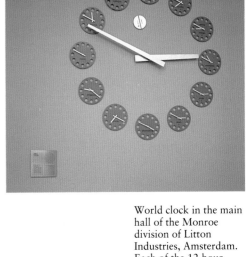

World clock in the main
hall of the Monroe
division of Litton
Industries, Amsterdam.
Each of the 12 hour
'dots' is a clock that gives
the corresponding time
at other Litton branches.

Design concept for the
renovation of the Dutch Railway Museum, Utrecht. For
logistic reasons of space, the
auditorium hangs as a tilted
box in the main hall. Designed
in association with the design
office of Donald Janssen,
The Hague. Photographer:
Fridtjof Versnel.

By Deborah Sussman

Reflections on Signs Past

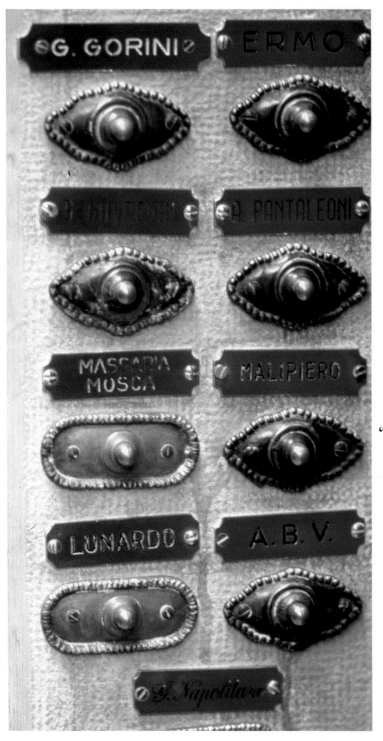

When did I fall in love with words and symbols on buildings and graphic images on the streets and rail lines that connected them? Perhaps it was as a child, riding the subways from Brooklyn to New York and seeing landmarks appear after emerging from the underground of DeKalb Avenue and downtown Brooklyn. Signs like *SQUIBB* appeared, as though the toothpaste tube had grown gigantic and attached itself to the tower, or the mystifying and frightening billboard *BELIEVE IN THE LORD JESUS CHRIST AND THOU SHALT BE SAVED* that announced one's arrival on the bridge over the East River. When the train descended underground again there were a series of stations with evocative names like Canal Street or Cortlandt Street suggesting other times, and early Dutch settlers whose lives helped shape the city. These names were rendered in tile and knit into the subway walls with patterns and mosaics that seemed inevitable and eternal, and in retrospect, "civic." The graphics of the New York subway provided a system of clues that helped frame the experience of traveling from my family and its homogeneous residential core to the great hub of the city. Many signals performed their public choreography, culminating in little red and green light bulbs overhead that marked the pedestrian routes along the turmoil of the 42nd Street underground.

Deborah Sussman is president of Sussman/ Prejza & Co., Inc. in Culver City, CA. She began her career an art director at the office of Charles and Ray Eames, and has since developed an extensive list of clients in the field of environmental graphic design, including Hasbro, Walt Disney World, and The U.S. Olympic Games. She is a member of the Alliance Graphique International and a past director of The American Institute of Graphic Arts.

Later I got to travel across the U.S. by railroad where the signals and signs along the tracks, as well as those hanging under spirited and welcoming station canopies identified the lines on the exotic cross-country routes. Even little detailed messages inside the nobly furnished compartments, added up to a visual culture filled with suggestion, memory, anticipation, discovery, and delight.

By the time that my work (plus a passion for exploration) led to my first Atlantic "crossing," by ship, I had become addicted to photographing every graphic signal that struck my eye. In Europe–as in Mexico, and later in Asia–my Exacta recorded thousands of images that strove to capture the moment and the place. Using the lens as a third eye, I discovered calligraphy floating on the windows of cafés in Holland, "eternal" porce-lain flowers on gravestones in the south of France; meticulously wrought bell ringers of brass in Italian apartments and German hallways; street numbers crafted in a way never seen on the streets of American cities. I was mesmerized by murals of tile that "signed" cafés in Madrid, and by the still-life school of street art painted on glass in the classic food shops of Paris.

My graphic world expanded to include the rhythms and patterns of brick and timber in southern Germany and Holland; the grids of windows on industrial buildings along canals; the colors of villages and cities so specific that their very names were "one" (Siena); the texture of fields that had been farmed and planted a certain way for generations. Capturing "a certain slant of light" at times could evoke a sense of place and climate so powerfully that even now I can smell the aroma that was there.

My hungry camera did not differentiate between "graphic" and "other"–everything on the streetscape called me and I responded, falling in love with the immediacy of the marketplace, the intimacy of cemeteries, and the ingenuity of communal celebrations. I photographed costumed parades where political commentary was displayed in gesture, music, dialect and makeup. I followed gypsies as they silently honored a dead queen, placing flowers on her grave. Street vendors became the subjects of my portraits and eventually their art became my influence. Recording the visual language of the street became a mission, a rite of passage to the world of Signs and Spaces that now commands my mind, heart, and soul.

The most profound inspirations for Deborah Sussman's work are revealed in her travel photographs that describe an entire world of graphics– designed to be read, to be used, to cultivate, to commemorate, to make places and define spaces.

Cloud and Gehshan Associates, Inc.

622 South 10th Street
Philadelphia, PA 19147
215/829-9414

Principals:
Jerome Cloud
Virginia Gehshan

Year Founded: 1986
Size of Firm: 7

Airlink computer hardware identity/ animation, for Hillier Technologies Group, Princeton, New Jersey, and Bresslergroup,

Philadelphia, Pennsylvania. Design Director and Designer: Jerome Cloud; Computer Illustration: Kent Massey.

Banner design for the Opera Company of Philadelphia/Luciano Pavarotti International Voice Competition. Designer: Jerome Cloud; Design assistance: Brad Kear; Photographer: Tom Crane.

Virginia Gehshan, Ann McDonald and Jerome Cloud, Cloud and Gehshan Associates, Inc.

Identity and sign design for Pilothouse, a Philadelphia waterfront store selling nautical books, charts and related paraphernalia. Design Director: Virginia Gehshan; Designer: Jerome Cloud; Photographer: Tom Crane.

Key Clients:
AT&T,
Ayers Saint Gross,
Bell of Pennsylvania,
Bank of Delaware,
Ewing Cole Cherry,
Franklin Institute,
Garden State Park,
The Hillier Group,
University of Maryland,
Meadowlands
Racetrack, Mellon Bank,
Nutri-System,
Pennsylvania
Convention Center,
University of
Pennsylvania,
Philadelphia Orchestra,
Prudential Property
Company, Thompson,
Ventulett Stainback &
Associates Inc., Tremont
Plaza Hotel, Wallace
Roberts & Todd,
Vanguard Group,
Zoological Society of
Philadelphia.

Cloud and Gehshan Associates, Inc.

Cloud and Gehshan is committed to expressing the distinctive and memorable identity of each client and project. The Philadelphia-based firm stresses the importance of context in their work, taking cues from the audience, architecture and landscape. Their design aims to humanize the built environment, using the resources of humor, inventive form and color. An additional priority, for large and complex assignments, is answering diverse parameters with clarity and continuity. Projects which demonstrate their ability to meet these goals include directional signage for the Philadelphia Zoo, environmental design for Baltimore's University Center, interpretive panels for Market Street East in Philadelphia and the identity and signage for the Pennsylvania Convention Center.

Signage for the Tremont Plaza Hotel, Baltimore, Maryland. Architects: Ayers Saint Gross, Baltimore; Design Director: Virginia Gehshan; Designers: Virginia Gehshan, Ann McDonald; Photographer, Tom Crane.

Logo for McIntosh Inns designed for numerous print and signage applications. Design Director: Virginia Gehshan; Designer: Jerome Cloud.

Kiosk for Philadelphia College of Textiles and Science is expressly made to accommodate student notices and postings. Clients: Philadelphia College of Textiles and Science, and Wallace Roberts & Todd.

Design Director: Virginia Gehshan; Designer: Jerome Cloud; Photographer: Tom Crane.

Campus map and signage program for Bryn Mawr College, Bryn Mawr, Pennsylvania. Detail of sign post. Design Director: Virginia Gehshan; Designer: Ann McDonald;

Map Designers: Jerome Cloud, Ann McDonald; Map Illustrator: Stacey Lewis; Photographer: Tom Crane.

Logo for Peoples State Bank. Design Director: Virginia Gehshan; Designers: Annette Vander, Jerome Cloud.

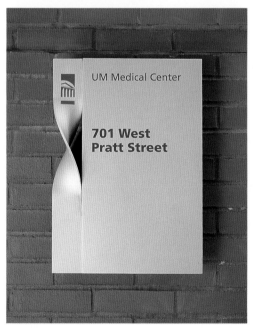

Environmental graphics and signage for University Center, a newly named district in the heart of Baltimore. Clients: University of Maryland at Baltimore, University of Maryland Medical System and Wallace Roberts & Todd, Philadelphia. Design Director: Virginia Gehshan; Designers: Jerome Cloud, Ann McDonald; Modelmaker: Brad Kear; Landscape Architecture: Wallace Roberts & Todd; Photographer: Tom Crane.

**Cloud and Gehshan
Associates, Inc.**

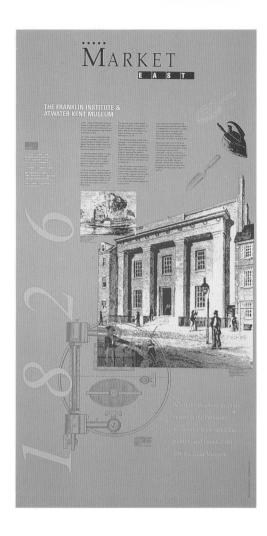

Identity and signage
for Pennsylvania
Convention Center, a
facility incorporating
the only remaining
single-span train shed
in the U.S. Clients:
Thompson, Ventulett
Stainback & Associates
and the Pennsylvania
Convention Center
Authority.

Design Directors:
Jerome Cloud,
Virginia Gehshan;
Designers: Jerome
Cloud, Ann McDonald;
Design Team:
Bradford Kear,
Annette Vander;
Modelmakers:
Brad Kear,
Chris Piccin.

Logo for T Squared
Architects. Designer:
Jerome Cloud.

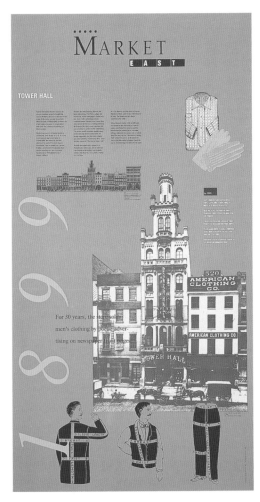

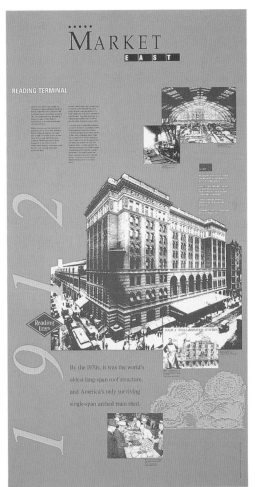

Display panels and transit shelter environmental signage design for Market Street renovation project, Philadelphia. The information is layered: those passing by quickly see a splash of color and a large date; those walking by see headlines, text and images; those waiting for buses have a variety of information to read. The fifteen different original panels are divided into themes of transportation, commerce, and architecture. Clients: The Delta Group, Philadelphia, and City of Philadelphia, Department of Streets; Design Concept: Virginia Gehshan; Design Director: Jerome Cloud; Designer: Ann McDonald; Historical Consultant: Robert Goldstein; Researchers: Ann McDonald, Virginia Gehshan, Pamela Pharr; Copywriter: James Smart.

GardenState
P · A · R · K

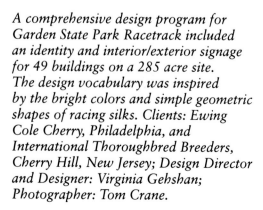

Entrance identification
sign, Garden State Park
Racetrack.

Grandstand colonnade
entrance and detail of
backstretch sign, Garden
State Park Racetrack.

Decorative and
informational signage
for the Teletheater
at the Meadowlands
Racetrack. Design
program also included
major exterior
identification signs.

Client: Ewing Cole
Cherry, Philadelphia;
Design Director:
Virginia Gehshan:
Designer: Ann McDonald;
Photographer:
James D'Addio.

*A comprehensive design program for
Garden State Park Racetrack included
an identity and interior/exterior signage
for 49 buildings on a 285 acre site.
The design vocabulary was inspired
by the bright colors and simple geometric
shapes of racing silks. Clients: Ewing
Cole Cherry, Philadelphia, and
International Thoroughbred Breeders,
Cherry Hill, New Jersey; Design Director
and Designer: Virginia Gehshan;
Photographer: Tom Crane.*

The challenge of the "Meet the Keeper" signage program was to create a flexible, changeable, reusable sign system at rock bottom cost for a summer program of different events. The whole system was designed and fabricated in 7 weeks. Bright colors and simple cutout animal shapes help in wayfinding to zoo areas. Client: Zoological Society of Philadelphia; Design Director: Virginia Gehshan; Designer: Jerome Cloud; Design Associate: Annette Vander; Detailing: Gary Lowe; Photographer, Tom Crane.

Logo for Intermission performing arts shop. Designer: Jerome Cloud.

Donald Janssen Ontwerpers

*Koningin Emmakade 199
NL2518 JP The Hague
Holland
070 34 64 232*

*Principal:
Donald Janssen*

*Year Founded: 1980
Size of Firm: 9*

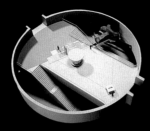

A 1:50 scale model of an underground station of the Dutch Railways at Rotterdam includes an excavated old town wall dating from 1340. The wall was incorporated into the architectural design as a line from past to present.

Client: Municipality of Rotterdam, Department for Archeological Research. Designers: Jan Hubert, Donald Janssen; Photographer: Jan Zweerts.

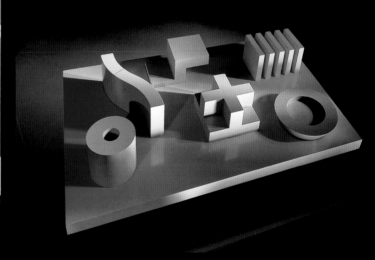

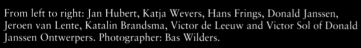

From left to right: Jan Hubert, Katja Wevers, Hans Frings, Donald Janssen, Jeroen van Lente, Katalin Brandsma, Victor de Leeuw and Victor Sol of Donald Janssen Ontwerpers. Photographer: Bas Wilders.

Photographs of a model used as a brochure illustration for Océ Nederland b.v. printing and publishing systems. Designer: Jan Hubert; Photographer: Reinier Gerritsen.

To celebrate "100 Years of Esso," removable exhibits were designed for a touring exhibition. Client: Esso Nederland; Designer: Jan Hubert.

Key Clients:
Dutch Railway Museum,
Esso Nederland,
ING Bank,
London Transport
Museum,
The Mauritshuis,
Ministry for Housing,
Regional Development
and the Environment,
Bureau Rijksbouwmeester,
The Hague;
Ministry of Welfare,
Health and
Cultural Affairs,
The Hague; Museon,
Museum New Land,
Museum of
North Brabant,
Municipal Museum
of the Hague,
Municipal Works
Department of
Rotterdam,
Nijgh & Van Ditmar
Educatief,
Postal Museum,
The Royal Dutch Post.

Donald Janssen Ontwerpers

For the Museon, The Hague, a complete layout of the Geology exhibition rooms was designed. Here, an information panel depicts 17 separate geologic elements based around a central floor scale model. Designers: Donald Janssen, Norma van Rees.

Donald Janssen set up his office in 1980, in the Dutch capital of the Hague, an area rich in design history. In the 1920s, Dutch artists pioneered the modernist concept of a total design scheme encompassing everything from graphics to architecture. In the post-WWII period, Holland has been a leader in putting such ideas into practice and Janssen is a committed advocate. Eschewing the naturalistic recreations of period settings common in contemporary historical museums, Janssen calls for an honest and unsentimental treatment of objects; he chooses to show the naked truth of artifacts, stripped of all illusionistic references to an original "context" that can never accurately be recaptured. Skilled in both industrial and graphic design, Janssen has created total design programs for numerous museums in Holland and the United Kingdom. His office uses a team approach to conceptualize the form and content of a diverse number of projects–from exhibition furniture to architectural signage–and then manages their execution from start to finish.

One of a series of interactive, educational exhibits for the Omniversum at The Hague. Designer: Hans Frings; Photographer: Jan Zweerts.

Series of CD label and package designs. Municipal Museum of The Hague (Music Department), The Hague, 1988. Designer: Jan Hubert; Photographer: Gerrit Schreurs.

The redesign of the Historical Museum of The Hague made extensive use of museum showcases. The modular design of the system permits each element to be connected with text panels in different configurations.

The system was manufactured in glass, granite (Rosa Porinho), MDF and aluminium. Photographer: Gerrit Schreurs.

"Portraits in Miniature," a touring exhibition of works in the National Museum Mauritshuis, is presented in specially designed, dimly lit (50 lux) showcases that are easy to set up. Designer: Victor the Leeuw; Photographer: Gerrit Schreurs.

At the entrance of the
gallery a floor plan
and general information
about the museum greets
visitors. Museum text
on curved wall leads into
the space.

Donald Janssen Ontwerpers designed
a complete redisplay program for
the Dutch Railway Museum, using
steel and glass as primary construction
materials. Open spaces and clean
lighting are effective complements to
the polished surfaces and strong colors.
The system included all information
panels and directional signage, as well
as floor maps of specific locations.
Designers: Donald Janssen, Paul
Mijksenaar, Hans Frings, Jan Hubert;
Photographer: Fridtjof Versnel.

Office signposting
system for the
Dutch Railways.
Client: Articon b.v.,
Amersfoort;
Designer: Jan Hubert;
Photographer:
Jan Zweerts.

The redesign of the
Museum of North
Brabant included
a completely new layout
as well as all printed
matter, such as catalogs,
posters and stationery.
Entrance sign to the
museum is made from
glass and stone.

Designers: Donald
Janssen, Jan Hubert,
Victor de Leeuw,
Hans Frings;
Photographers:
Fridtjof Versnel,
Jan Hubert.

For the Dutch Postal Museum, Janssen designed a fold-up directional plan that included explanatory texts. Designers: Donald Janssen, Norma van Rees; Photographer: Gerrit Schreurs.

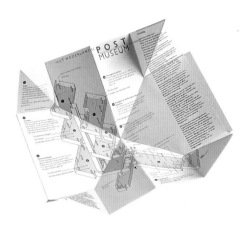

Herentoiletten
Koffiekamer
Telefoon

Signposting system for the Dutch Postal Museum. Solid aluminium plate. Dutch Postal Museum, The Hague, 1985. Designer: Donald Janssen; Photographer: Jan Zweerts.

As part of the redesign of the Dutch Postal Museum, the Historical Department area includes a central three-dimensional map of the region. Floor plans permit ease of access through what is a usually crowded thoroughfare. Display cases in the Historical Department have roller casters on them, permitting them to be changed and moved easily. Sloping, curvilinear walls are designed to enclose specific display areas, yet are not higher than the line of vision. Designer: Donald Janssen; Photographers: Jan Zweerts, Fridtjof Versnel.

"Aart's Paradise" was an exhibition designed at the Government Pavilion for the International Horticultural Show "Floriade."

Client: Ministry of Agriculture, Nature Conservation and Fisheries, The Hague; Designers: Donald Janssen, Jan Hubert, Hans Frings, Jeroen van Lente; Photographer: Jan Zweerts.

Permanent exhibition for the Roosevelt Study Center, Middelburg. The exhibition displays a history of the President and his wife, Eleanor Roosevelt. Information panels are hung as banners on triple-pronged display posts. Designer: Victor de Leeuw; Photographer: Fridtjof Versnel.

Interior layout
plan of London
Transport Museum.

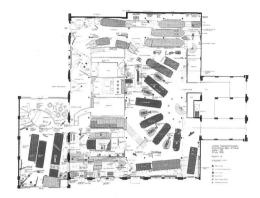

In cooperation with Dry Butlin &
Bicknell, Architects, Donald Janssen
Ontwerpers designed an entirely
new permanent redisplay and layout
for the London Transport Museum.
The system included exhibition
furniture, interactive exhibits, audio-
visual touchscreen information units
and all graphic design. Left, four
scale models (1:10) of showcases in
combination with photopanels. In
the foreground is a model for one of
the touchscreen monitors. Designers:
Donald Janssen, Jan Hubert, Jeroen
van Lente, Hans Frings; Photographer:
Gerrit Schreurs.

Rough design
sketches for steel
and glass museum
showcases. Designer:
Donald Janssen.

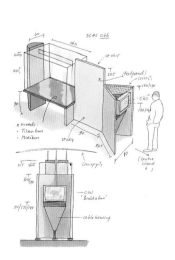
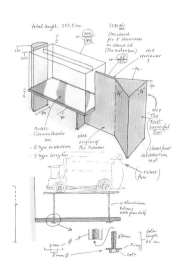
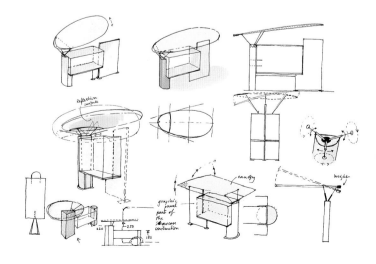

Carbone Smolan Associates

22 West 19th Street
New York, NY 10011
212/807-0011

Principals:
Ken Carbone
Leslie Smolan

Year Founded: 1977
Size of Firm: 25

Ken Carbone and Leslie Smolan, principals of Carbone Smolan Associates.
Photographer: Doug Menuez/Reportage.

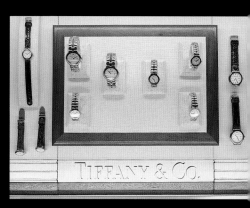

*Global display program for Tiffany &
Company is based on a modular system
that is adaptable to a variety of in-store
conditions. The program reflects details
of casework designed for the Fifth
Avenue flagship store by Stanford White.
Stainless steel, cherry wood and linen are
the primary materials used. Design
Associates: NBBJ/Retail Concepts;
Photographer: Elliot Kaufman.*

Key Clients:
Citibank,
Cleary Gottlieb
Steen & Hamilton,
Etablissement Public du
Grand Louvre,
The Museum of
Modern Art,
The Pierpont
Morgan Library,
Tiffany & Company,
Pei Cobb Freed
Architects, Kohn
Pederson Fox, Kohn
Pederson Fox Interior
Architects,
Hardy Holzman
Pfieffer Associates,
Voorsanger and
Associates.

Carbone Smolan Associates

GRAND LOUVRE

Carbone Smolan Associates
Signalétique du Grand Louvre
Programme Design

Cover Design for
Carbone Smolan
Associates' winning
proposal for the
Grand Louvre's
international signage
competition.

Carbone Smolan Associates emphasizes innovative design that is intelligent, accessible and distinctive. They maintain creative vitality by seeking design projects that use the full range of their talents. Among the services they offer are corporate identity, print communications, book design, packaging and promotion. In addition, their work in environmental graphics has gained them an international reputation, attracting an elite clientele including major corporations, cultural institutions, hotels and retail establishments. Their goal is to uncover the creative opportunities in the challenges presented to them by clients and architects, and with them, to build partnerships to achieve impressive results. They excel in projects that require simple yet dramatic solutions to complex problems, creating a successful balance between architecture and operations.

Carbone Smolan's visitor information system and signage program for the Etablissement Public du Grand Louvre guides five million visitors annually, starting at the "new front door" of the I.M. Pei pyramid, and continuing throughout various galleries. Photographers: Phillippe de Potestad, George Kamper.

Various fabrication techniques were used in the signage program, including hand-carved letters in marble, glass and stainless steel directional signs, aluminum and silkscreen orientation maps, and bead-blast stainless steel letters. A tri-color coding system is used for vertical circulation.

The French typeface Granjon is used throughout the system, including six-inch letters carved in the marble walls of the pyramid's reception area.

Aluminum and silkscreen maps located on the exterior of the museum guide visitors to the main entrance.

Main visitor information wall and reception area. Each wing of the museum is identified by its historical name and masterpieces included in its collection. Video monitors display notices about current exhibitions and daily activities in six languages.

Exterior sign/sculpture
for 2015 Main Street in
Greenwich, Connecticut
is cut out of one curved
4' x 8' sheet of aluminum.

Exterior sign/sculpture
at the main entrance to
Tallyrand Office Park
is composed of eight
10-ft. "T"-shaped panels
that graduate from green
to blue or blue to green,
depending on the
direction you approach
them. Photographer:
Richard Marin.

The Market at Citicorp
Center exterior signage
is a 24-ft. long "canopy"
that is cantilevered off
the building facade. Ten
triangular panels give
the sign visual impact
without added weight.

Each of the panels is
fabricated from
perforated aluminum
and finished in
automotive paint.

Exterior and interior architectural signage program for The Pierpont Morgan Library, New York. The signs are made of brass with three custom-finished patinas hand-applied on a special textured background. The program includes an orientation map, directional signs, gallery identification, code signage and benefactors' identification. Photographer: Paul Warchol.

Free-standing sign located on the information desk in the main lobby describing the library's admission policy.

Identification sign located at the entrance to Mr. Morgan's private study.

Stainless steel and
acrylic menu display.

The interior architectural signage
program for Cleary Gottlieb Steen &
Hamilton includes permanent and
changeable signs that are based on
the colors of the interior spaces.
The changeable signs are made of
satin bronze, etched and paint-filled
type with painted acrylic supports.
Photographer: Whitney Cox.

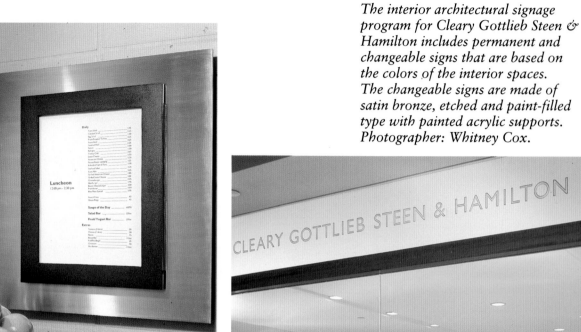

Office identification
signs can be changed as
required while a hidden
magnetic device provides
a look of permanance.

The name of the firm is
carved into a glass panel
at the main entrance.

A simple painted
acrylic name plaque
for secreterial stations
uses the same colors,
typeface and details
as seen throughout
the program.

Museum of Modern Art exterior and interior architectural signage program. Various sign components feature fiberglass panels with stainless steel letters, banners, stainless steel and glass poster displays, donor recognition panels and multicolored signage for the museum cafe. Photographer: Mark Greenburg.

Exterior banners display
the museum's name
and current exhibitions.

Communication Arts Inc.

1112 Pearl Street
Boulder, CO
80302
303/447-8202

Principals:
Henry Beer
Richard A.Foy
Janet A. Martin

Year Founded: 1973
Size of Firm: 35

Richard A. Foy, Janet A. Martin, Henry Beer, principals of Communication Arts Inc.

The City and County of Denver's Sports Complex/Mile High Stadium has "goal posts" to beckon and orient visitors. Design Principal: Richard A. Foy; Designers: Mark Tweed, Phil Reed; Project Director: Gary Kushner.

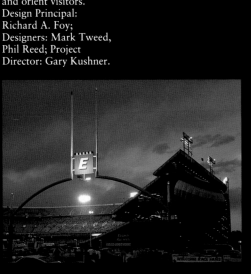

Design and signage program for The Minnesota Timberwolves Arena, known as the Target Center, encompassed exterior facade, interior signage and concession areas. Design Principal: Richard A. Foy; Designers: Mark Tweed, Margaret Sewell; Project Director: John Ward; Architect: KMR Architects; Photographer: Steven Bergerson.

Communication Arts Inc.

Key Clients:
CenterMark Properties,
Donahue Schriber,
Disney Development
Company,
The Edward J.
DeBartolo Corporation,
Equity Properties,
The Jerde Partnership,
The Linpro Company,
The MacArthur
Foundation,
Martin Marietta
Aerospace,
Paramount
Communications,
Prudential Property
Company,
The Rouse Company,
US West, Inc.,
Western Development
Corporation.

Logo for Fiddler's Green
Outdoor Amphitheatre,
Denver, Colorado.

The Sportsgirl Centre in
Melbourne is a four-level
retail atrium, flagship
store and corporate
headquarters for the
Sportsgirl chain. The
terrazzo pattern for the
lower level, called the
"energy level," creates a
sense of dynamism and
activity to draw shoppers
to the smaller, one-of-a-
kind designer shops
located downstairs.

Design Principal:
Henry Beer; Designer:
David A. Brown; Project
Director: John Ward;
Architect: Anthony
Belluschi Architects;
Photographer:
R. Greg Hursley, Inc.

Communication Arts has built an international reputation wtih large-scale projects that depend on acceptance from a broad public. The firm's wide-ranging work balances curiosity, emotion and intellect with a strong grasp of real-world needs and restrictions of clients, users, schedules and budgets. Founded in 1973, its philosophy is that design transforms the goals, concepts and wishes of a company or institution into things the public will use, understand and experience. Building on the spirit of Charles Eames (mentor of the firm's founders Henry Beer and Richard Foy), Communication Arts has developed expertise in architectural, interior, industrial and graphic design. Projects include corporate identity and marketing communications as well as environmental design programs for the retail, entertainment, development and hospitality industries.

University of Colorado's
Research Park entry
signs and sculptures
were carved from local
stone and etched with
gold leaf depicting
scientific and
mathematical symbols.
Design Principal:
Richard A. Foy;
Designers: Phil Reed,
Patricia Van Hook;
Project Director: Gary
Kushner; Architect: Gage
Davis International.

Western Development Corporation's Gurnee Mills outlet mall is the world's largest, with over two million square feet of space. Every detail of the project signage and design refers to some vernacular form, idea or material attributable to the American Midwest, such as state fairs, roadside food stands, and agricultural structures and icons. Design Principal: Henry Beer; Design Team: Bryan Gough, Paul Mack, Jr., Larry Weeks, Lydia Young, Todd Cail, Scott Bonnenfant, Mark Tweed, Hugh Enockson, Tamia Wardle, Zina Castanuela, Lynn Williams; Project Director: John Ward; Architect: Cambridge Seven Associates; Photographer: R. Greg Hursley, Inc.

"Dine-O-Rama" food court takes its inspiration from America's love of automobiles. The ceiling was lighted and painted to simulate a night sky, under which antique cars serve as mobile retail units.

Design for Skinner Development Company's Carillon Point includes five 50-foot high carillons that act as beacons and navigational signage. They happily chime out every hour. Flag-bearing stanchions designed to resemble fishing poles mark the Marina's entrance gate. Design Principal: Henry Beer; Designers: Bryan Gough, David A. Shelton, David Tweed, Phil Reed; Project Director: Gary Kushner; Architect: The Callison Partnership; Photographer: R. Greg Hursley, Inc.

**Communication
Arts Inc.**

Communication Arts fashioned a "parabolic parasol pergola" that proceeds through an intricate garden geometry, connecting the office development with the retail core.

For The Rouse Company's Arizona Center, a signage and amenities program emphasized and enhanced the play of light and shade in the desert environment. Signage is embossed in the stucco structures, and takes advantage of the dramatic solar angles in this latitude. Colors are a cool counterpoint throughout. Design Principal: Henry Beer; Designers: Gary Kushner, David A. Shelton, Phil Reed, Patricia Van Hook; Landscape Architect: SWA Group; Architect: ELS Architects; Photographer: Dixi Carrillo.

The design program for St. Louis Union Station incorporates "See the Station by Rail" panels and directories that chronicle the history and people of the station. Client: The Rouse Company; Design Principal: Henry Beer; Designers: Gary Kushner, Doug Stelling, Mike Doyle, Steve Ericson, Bryan Gough, Mark Tweed, David Tweed, Paul Mack, Jr.; Architect: HOK; Photographer: William Mathis.

Lighting is the focal point of the vast arena/exhibition area and the new 5,600-seat Paramount Theatre.

Paramount Communications' renovation of Madison Square Garden focused on the modernization of the arena, two new restaurants, new private boxes, food courts, concession stands, restrooms and a complete signage and graphics program. Design Principal: Richard A. Foy; Design Team: Kevin Kearney, Bryan Gough, David A. Shelton, Guy Thornton, Margaret Sewell, David Tweed, Zina Castanuela, Rory McCarthy, Julie Wynn; Project Director: Gary Kushner; Project Architect: Ellerbe Becket; Photographer: R. Greg Hursley, Inc.

**Communication
Arts Inc.**

The sign for Eatz
food court serves as a
landmark for shoppers
as they navigate three
levels and four wings.

*Santa Monica Place's entrance utilizes a
profusion of light, architectural form
and color. Client: The Rouse Company;
Design Principal: Richard A. Foy;
Design Team: Mike Doyle, Paul Mack,
Jr., T. Keith Harley; Project Director:
John Ward; Architect: Ray Bailey
Architects; Photographers: Jerry Butts,
R. Greg Hursley, Inc.*

Detail of entrance
signage creates the effect
of letters seeming to
float overhead.

A monolithic entry sign that is gradated in pastels by day and edge-lit neon in three colors by night greets visitors to this retail center in Miami. Client: The Rouse Company; Design Principal: Henry Beer; Designers: Gary Kushner, Chi Ming Kan; Architect: Benjamin Thompson Associates; Photographer: R. Greg Hursley, Inc.

Signage program for Rivercenter in San Antonio for the Edward DeBartolo Corporation is enhanced by ribbon and banner motifs. Design Principal: Henry Beer; Design Team: Bryan Gough, Mike Doyle, John Ward, David Garrett; Architect: Urban Design Group; Photographer: R. Greg Hursley, Inc.

Logo, menu and matchbook design for Restaurant Picasso at the Lodge at Cordillera.

By Takenobu Igarashi

Designing Out the Garbage

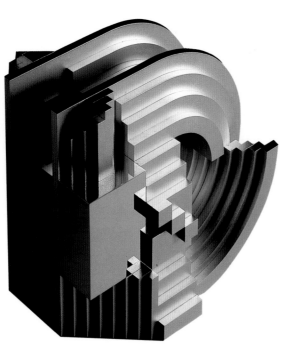

Igarashi's "D" alphabet sculpture, cast in two-toned aluminum and gold-plated brass, was designed and created for the cover of Domus Magazine. Client: Domus Monthly Review of Architecture Interiors Design Art Magazine, Milano, Italy; Photographer: Mitsumasa Fujitsuka.

When one is designing or creating something it is easier to always consider the risks that are inherently connected to destroying the Earth's environment. People are becoming more sensitive about the environment to the extent that many of us agree humans are carrying out the destruction of the planet. As designers, we are only too aware of the damage and are thus pushing to reform the usage of signs. Even though it is obvious that the essential function of signs is to indicate places and to provide people with necessary information for the purpose of movement, there nevertheless is an excess of color, shape and words that calls for a reinvestigation of "signs."

I think we are approaching an era that demands designers strive to satisfy the maximum limits of a function with minimum effort and materials. This ensurance of high quality would then call attention to methods that resist wasteful use of precious resources. With these concepts in mind, I could simply state that my attitude is such that I try to realize the high cultural quality of fine art and the functional, simple intimacy of design in my environmental signs. The alphabet sculptures, for example, were created with the intention of having them become monuments for the environment emphasizing the pleasure of sight while maintaining its inherent function as symbols, characters for reading.

With this said, I implore everyone to find a way and do their part, no matter how small, to rid the Earth of its garbage.

Takenobu Igarashi established a graphic design studio soon after college and expanded to include sculpture, environmental and product design. Working between two- and three-dimensional mediums, Igarashi's sculpture, particularly his alphabet series, liberates signage from its constraints of merely being a directional indicator to something of simple, functional beauty. His work has appeared throughout Europe, the United States and Japan.

The blue of the sea and white-capped waves were the inspiration for the signage and floor tile design for the Tokyo Metropolitan Government's Tokyo Port Management Office. Architect: Minoru Takeyama; Collaborating Designers: Takenobu Igarashi, Kazuhiro Hayase. Photographer: Nacasa & Partners, Inc.

**Debra Nichols
Design**

468 Jackson Street
San Francisco, CA
94111
415/788-0766

Principal: Debra Nichols

Year Founded: 1991
Size of Firm: 5

Debra Nichols, principal of Debra Nichols Design.

NEWMARK

The graphics scope for the Seattle,
Washington-based Newmark includes
the design of their logo, exterior and
interior signage, exterior color design
and interior accessories such as light
fixtures, shopping bags, etc. Client:
Intrawest, Seattle, Washington;
Senior Designer: Debra Nichols*.

*Asterisk indicates
projects designed while
an Associate Partner
and Director of Graphic
Design at Skidmore,
Owings & Merrill,

Key Clients:
Anshen + Allen
Architects,
Brayton/Hughes Design
Studio, Club Source,
De Stefano + Partners,
Flood Partners, Golden
State Warriors, IBM,
Maguire/Thomas
Partners, Newhall Land
and Farming Company,
The John Buck
Company, University of
California Berkeley,
University of California
Davis, University of
Southern California,
Cesar Pelli and
Associates, Legorreta
Arquitectos,
Redevelopment Agency
of San Jose, Equitable
Real Estate, Honorway
Investment Corporation,
The Yarmouth Group,
Mitchell/Giurgola
Architects, Orlando
Diaz-Azcuy, Keating
Mann Jernigan Rottet,
Sears Tower
Management.

Debra Nichols Design

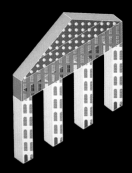

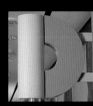

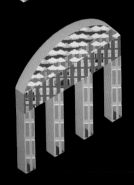

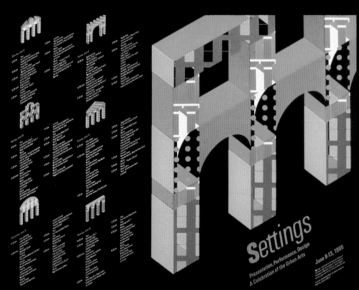

Debra Nichols makes graphics an integral part of an architectural vision. She conceives of signage not as an independent communications system installed in a building, but as an intimate extension of its architecture. As Associate Partner and Director of Graphic Design at Skidmore, Owings & Merrill for fifteen years, Nichols helped forge a unique graphic design office in the context of that firm's architectural practice. In addition to SOM projects, her studio received outside commissions for graphics from developers and architects including the Disney Headquarters in Burbank (designed by Michael Graves) and Solana (the Texas business park designed by Ricardo Legorreta and Mitchell/Giurgola). Since founding her own firm in 1991, Nichols has continued to emphasize a collaboration between architecture and graphics where signage extends the spirit of the setting or, in some cases, suggests an effective counterpoint to it.

Graphic identity and banner program application for "Settings," an Urban Arts Celebration concurrent with the 1985 AIA National Convention in San Francisco. Clients: San Francisco Arts Commission, The American Institute of Architects/S.F.; Senior Designer: Debra Nichols*

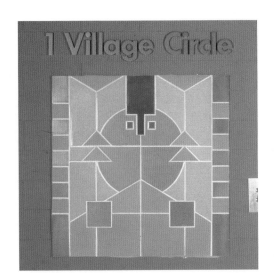

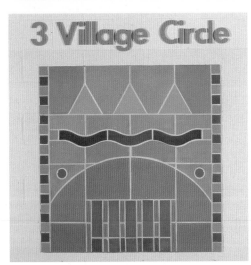

*The signage masterplan for the
Solana office park in Westlake, Texas
encompasses a 900 acre, 7 million
square foot facility. Applications include
site directional signage, exterior, interior,
informational, traffic regulatory, code
and decorative elements. Clients:
Maguire/Thomas Partners, Westlake,
Texas and IBM, New York;
Senior Designer: Debra Nichols*;
Photographer: Wes Thompson.*

Large metal animals act as both art, landmarks and guideposts marking major and secondary intersections. The animals are inspired by native Southwestern art and are made of oxidized bronze and aluminum painted hot pink, yellow and turquoise.

**Debra Nichols
Design**

Signage characters for the Solana Child Development Center, Westlake, Texas include logo design and signs which distinguish classrooms using images of small indigenous animals. Client: Maguire/Thomas Partners, Westlake, Texas; Senior Designer: Debra Nichols.

Entrance signage for 88 Kearny Street, San Francisco Federal Savings. The signage bands wrap the base of the building, and the form is repeated in poster holders designed for promotional posters in display windows. Client: San Francisco Federal Savings/Jaymont Properties; Senior Designer: Debra Nichols*; Photographer: Jane Lidz.

Solana

CHILD

DEVELOPMENT CENTER

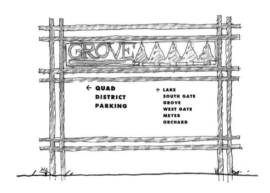

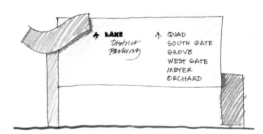

Campus signage masterplan of directional, identification and informational signage for University of California, Davis. The imagery refers to physical or historical characteristics of the campus. Symbols are used as organizational devices to indicate districts as destinations. Client: U. C. Davis, Office of Architects and Engineers; Designer: Debra Nichols.

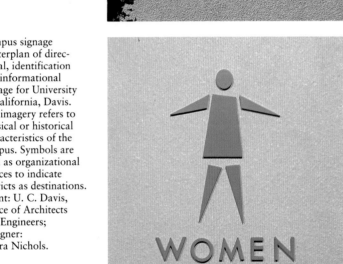

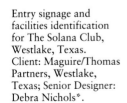

Entry signage and facilities identification for The Solana Club, Westlake, Texas. Client: Maguire/Thomas Partners, Westlake, Texas; Senior Designer: Debra Nichols*.

Hotel signage plaques for Dallas-Solana Marriott, Westlake, Texas. Client: Maguire/ Thomas Partners; Senior Designer: Debra Nichols*; Photographer: Wes Thompson.

**Debra Nichols
Design**

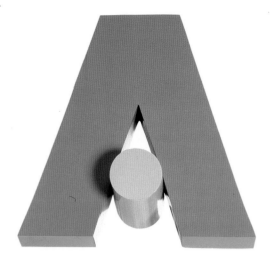

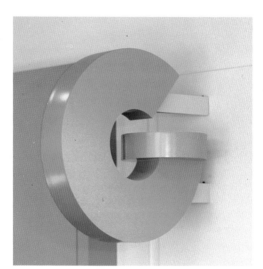

Model for exterior site
signage component.

*The graphic system for the Kaiser Medical
Office Building in Vallejo, California
includes exterior and interior signage
program for the Medical Facility Campus
entry, extensive interior directional signage
using large-scale letterforms to identify
wings off of the major corridor. Client:
Kaiser Permanente, Vallejo, California;
Senior Designer: Debra Nichols*;
Photographer: Nan Park.*

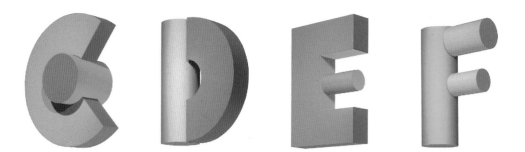

View of wing directory and "undulating" building directory walls at entrance to facility.

Gottschalk+Ash International

11 Bishop Street
Toronto, Ontario
Canada M5R 1N3
416/963-9717

Böcklinstrasse 26
Postfach 268
8032 Zürich
Switzerland
01-382-1850

2050 Rue Mansfield
Montréal, Quebec
Canada H3A 1Y9
514/844-1995

Principals:
Fritz Gottschalk
Stuart Ash
Peter Steiner
Helene L'Heureux

Year Founded: 1966
Size of Firm: 25

Detail of SkyDome
logo element
impressed into
concrete.

For the Stadium Corporation of
Ontario's SkyDome, the design consor-
tium of Gottschalk+Ash International
and Keith Muller+Associates developed
a comprehensive signage and way-
finding, visual identity, graphic design
and advertising display system.
SkyDome is the world's first solid
structure, retractable roof stadium.
Design Group: Gottschalk+Ash
International, Stuart Ash, Principal;
Designers: Peter Adam, Brenda
Tong, Katalin Kovats, Robert Jensen;
Industrial Design: Keith Muller
+Associates, Keith Muller, Principal;
Randy Johnson, Project Coordinator;
Designers: Larry Burak,
Davide Tonizzo, Joanna Crone,
Robert Ketchen, Ian Watson.

Key Clients:
Air Canada,
Akademischer
Reisedienst/.
Studentenwerk
Konstanz, Alcan,
Alrodo, Bank Leu,
Canada Post, Canadian
Museum of Nature,
Canadian Pacific,
Cantel, Chartered
Accountants of Canada,
City of Baar/SGA
Société Générale
d'Affichage, City of
Dietikon/SGA Société
Générale d'Affichage,
City of Toronto, City of
Zurich/Municipal Office
for Advertising,
Consumers Gas,
Forchbahn, Merck
Frosst, Neue Bank,
Petro Canada,
Plakatron, Prolitteris,
Rogers Communications
Inc., SkyDome, Stadler
Verlag, SZU Sihltal
Zurich Uetliberg Bahn,
Vereinsbank, Verit,
VHV/BCG Association
of Swiss Commercial
Banks, Victoria
Bayerische Vereinsbank.

Gottschalk+Ash
International

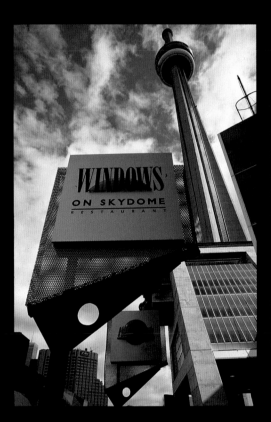

Exterior signs for
restaurants and bars
within the SkyDome.

G+A Gottschalk+Ash International labels its diverse services "strategic design," a phrase suggesting the firm's rigorously analytical approach to design. The firm's services encompass corporate identity, product development, packaging, print communications, signage and wayfinding programs. The firm stresses research, well considered design and quality control over flashy visuals. Gottschalk +Ash practices design as an international business capable of confronting economic realities as well as aesthetic subtleties. In partnership with the industrial design office of Keith Muller+Associates, Gottschalk+Ash produced a comprehensive design program for Toronto's SkyDome sports and entertainment complex. The project was self-financing: the team combined wayfinding with advertising billboards, the revenues from which paid for design and implementation costs. The SkyDome's $11 million yearly advertising revenues are double those of comparable facilities, with the integrated display advertising contributing $6 million a year.

Sample pages from
the identity guidelines
book developed for
use by other designers
and licensees of the
SkyDome image.

Interior of stadium shows modesty screen
and sign band providing orientation to
seating incorporating the identity
elements of sky, stars, sun and moon.
The modesty screen incorporates revenue
generating advertising, which offset
the cost of fabrication and continues to
generate long-term revenues.

SKYDOME

SkyDome "D" visual
identity and stationery
application.

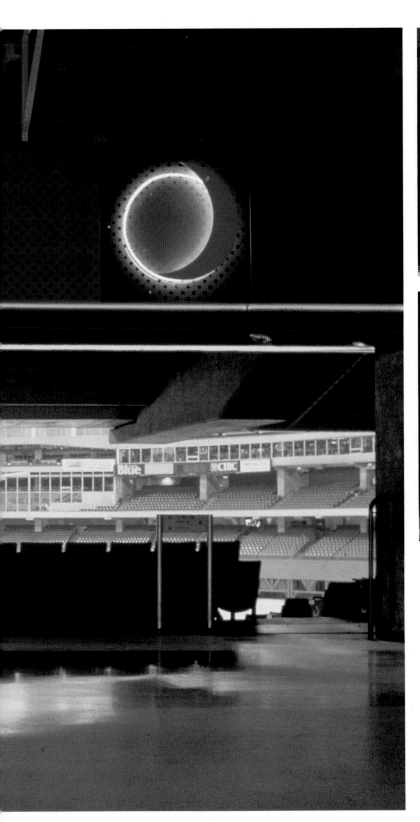

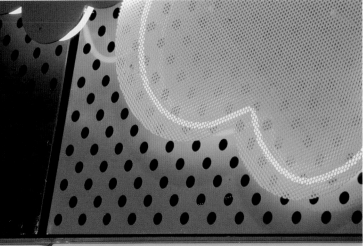

Details of sign band
"modesty screen"
showing use of perfor-
ated metal, neon and
colored enamel panels
for sky elements of
clouds and sun.

Detail of construction
hoarding for Bank Leu,
Switzerland. Designer:
Fritz Gottschalk.

Signage program and
identity for Scotiabank at
Scotia Plaza, for Campeau
Corporation/Bank of
Nova Scotia. Designers:
Stuart Ash, Joanne Lee,
Peter Adam.

Detail of billboard and
bench design; T-profile
is being applied as
a unifying structural
element.

Combination billboard
and seating area is
an integrated design
element.

*Station design and outdoor advertising
panels for Sihltal Uetliberg Bahn,
Zürich, Switzerland. When not used,
the advertising panels act as open
view windows for the station shelter.
Designers: Fritz Gottschalk, Erich Gross.*

System map indicating
PATH access in Toronto's
downtown core.

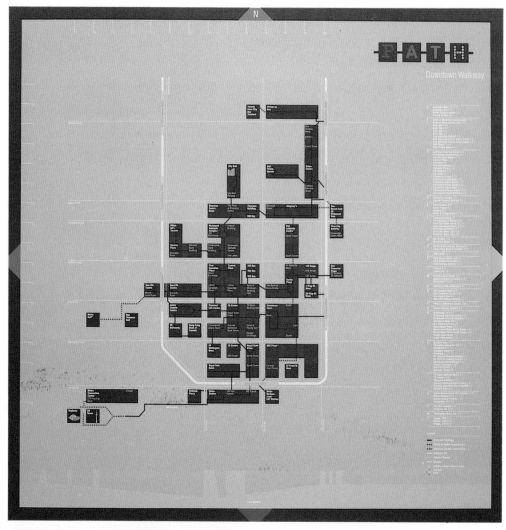

Prototype for station
marker pylon.

*PATH (Toronto Underground
Walkway System) development includes
identity and complete wayfinding
system for Toronto's core underground
shopping complex, which has approx-
imately six miles of pedestrian
walkways. Designers: Stuart Ash,
Peter Adam, Diane Castellan, Katalin
Kovats; Industrial Design: Keith
Muller+Associates, Principal, Keith
Muller; Designer: Merritt Price.*

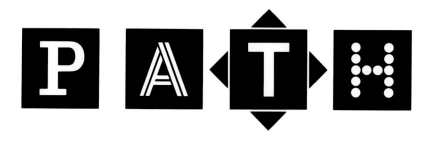

You are in:
First Canadian Place

South to:
TD Centre

Commercial Union T
Ernst & Young To
Royal Trust Tow

Typical PATH
directional signage.
Signs are porcelain
enamel finish on steel.

You are in:
First Canadian Place

South to:
TD Centre
  Commercial Union Tower
  Ernst & Young Tower
  Royal Trust Tower
  TD Bank Banking Hall
  Toronto Dominion Bank Tower

Two Twelve Associates, Inc.

596 Broadway
New York, NY
10012-3233
212/925-6885

Principals:
David Gibson
Sylvia Woodard
Juanita Dugdale

Associates:
Julie Marable
David Peters

Year Founded: 1980
Size of Firm: 12

An in-house interactive information service for CIGNA. Placed in kiosks throughout the corporate offices, the program offers an on-line employee handbook, daily transit information, cafeteria menus and company news. Design Director: Sylvia Woodard; Designer: Terrie Dunkelberger.

Campus directory for the Ohio University campus in Athens, Ohio. The design of this comprehensive system invokes the school's 00-year history and Georgian campus buildings. Design Directors: David Gibson, Sylvia Woodard; Designer: Jose Delano; Photographer: ake Wyman.

David Gibson, managing principal of Two Twelve Associates, Inc.

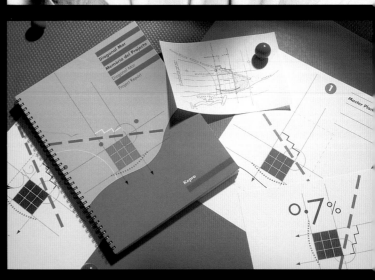

Diagonal Mar master plan report for a mixed-use development in Barcelona, Spain. The cover image is inspired by the architect's schematic plan of the project.

Client: Cooper Robertson + Partners; Design Director: David Gibson; Designers: Douglas Morris, Barbara Glauber; Photographer: Susan Wides.

Two Twelve Associates, Inc.

Company, Bechtel
Parsons/Brinkerhoff,
Chemical Bank, NA,
Citibank, NA,
Cooper Robertson +
Partners, Forest City
Dillon, Howard Needles
Tammen & Bergendoff,
Kevin Roche John
Dinkeloo and
Associates, Kohn
Pedersen Fox Associates,
Maryland Mass
Transit Administration,
Massachusetts
Department of Public
Works, Metropolitan
Transportation
Authority, Ohio
University, New York
Zoological Society,
Pfizer, Inc., Rockefeller
Center Management
Corp.,The Walt
Disney Company.

The Baltimore Waterfront
Promenade logo identifies
signs and interpretive
panels as part of a new
walkway along
Baltimore's harbor.
Client: Baltimore Harbor
Endowment; Design
Director: David Gibson;
Designers: Douglas
Morris, Julie Marable.

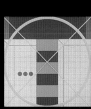

Two Twelve Associates, Inc., a
New York-based multidisciplinary
design firm, specializes in *public
information design,* the planning
and presentation of complex
information to large, broad-based audiences.
The firm creates signage systems by first looking
at the audience the signs will serve. Who will
use the signs? What will they want to know?
How will they expect signs to work?
Incorporating users and their needs into the
design process, Two Twelve starts by developing
a simple, intuitively understood wayfinding
strategy. Supporting this basic structure is
a sophisticated use of type, image, color and
materials that takes its visual cues from the
architectural, cultural and historical contexts of
the environment. Expertise developed through
the firm's work in two other disciplines,
publication and computer interface design,
further informs the signage design.

Gate sign for Rhode
Island's new T.F. Green
Airport. Strong colors
bring sophisticated style
to airport signage.
Client: Rhode Island
Department of
Transportation; Design
Directors: David Gibson,
Douglas Morris;
Designers: Nicholas
Grohe, Ben Goodman;
Architects: Howard
Needles Tammen &
Bergendoff.

A graphics program,
including maps,
directories and visitors'
guides, welcomes 12
million visitors a year to
the South Street Seaport
Museum and Market-
place. Outdoor
interpretive panels

describe the Museum's
collection of historic
ships. Design Director:
David Gibson;
Designers: Jose Delano,
Tracey Cameron,
Douglas Morris;
Map Illustration:
Lieu and Silks;

Kiosk Frame: Benjamin
Thompson Associates;
Photographer:
Jake Wyman.

**Two Twelve
Associates, Inc.**

Identity and outdoor
signage for Loeb
Boathouse lakefront
restaurant and boat rental
facility in New York's
Central Park. Designer:
David Gibson; Illustrator:
Christine Zelinsky.

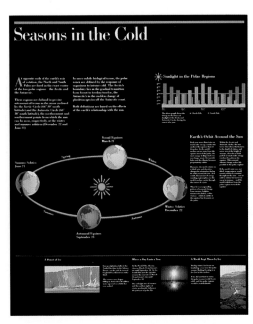

*The sign system and exhibit graphics
program for the New York Zoological
Society's Central Park Zoo combines the
sophistication of New York's Museum
Mile with a sense of fun and easy
accessibility for the Zoo's youngest
visitors. The program, which educates
and entertains, included design and
production of all directional and
orientation signs, visitor maps,
interpretive panels and animal
identifications. Design Director: David
Gibson; Designer: Tracey Cameron;
Architects: Kevin Roche John Dinkeloo
and Associates; Photographer: Peter
Aaron, Esto.*

Enameltec porcelain
enamel provided
superior full-color
reproduction for
interpretive plaques
combining text,
photography and
illustrations.

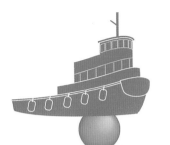

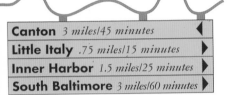

The Baltimore Waterfront Promenade signage program uses trailblazers, directional signs, mileposts, maps and interpretive graphic panels to define a pedestrian right-of-way running along Baltimore Harbor. Client: Baltimore Harbor Endowment; Design Directors: David Gibson, Douglas Morris; Designers: Julie Marable, Helene Benedetti; Architects: Cho, Wilks & Benn Architects; Photographer: Jake Wyman.

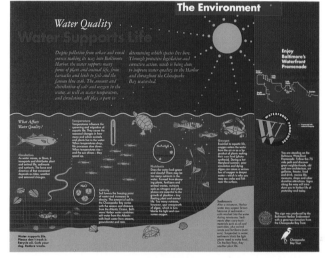

Illustration and color combine to create rich, multilayered interpretive panels that provide background information for people strolling along the Promenade. These panels focus on environmental issues; others describe the people of Baltimore, the growth of the city and the Harbor's history.

The sign system for the U.S. Courthouse at Foley Square, in New York City, consists of etched glass message panels attached to stainless steel plaques. The layering creates an interesting three-dimensional effect and allows the elegant incorporation of braille in its own field on the stainless steel.

The system is fully compliant with the Americans with Disabilities Act. Client: Kohn Pedersen Fox Associates; Design Director: David Gibson; Designer: Douglas Morris; Design Collaborators: Harakawa Sisco, Inc.

Identity and signage system design for The Millender Center in downtown Detroit. Developed by Forest City Dillon, the Center complex combines hotel, office, retail and parking space. The logo draws from the building's stair-step architecture and the intersection of several mass transit systems at the site. Design Director: David Gibson; Designers: Mark Koch, Randy Smith; Architects: The Ehrenkrantz Group; Photographer: Stan Reis.

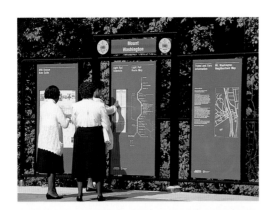

Passenger waiting areas feature maps both of the local neighborhoods and the complete Light Rail system.

The signage and information graphics program of the Baltimore Light Rail Line, created for the Maryland Mass Transit Administration (MTA), uses the MTA blue with yellow to identify the Light Rail line among the city's transit options. Consistent use of these vibrant colors helps the signs and stations to stand out in the busy urban environment. Design Director: David Gibson; Designer: Douglas Morris; Architects: Cho, Wilks & Benn Architects; Engineers: Parsons-Brinckerhoff-Morrison-Knudson; Photographer: Jake Wyman.

A unified color treatment encompasses all aspects of the Central Artery/Third Harbor Tunnel system from buildings and highway structures to signage. The Massachusetts Department of Public Works managed this $5 billion public works project in Boston.

Design Director: David Gibson; Designers: Douglas Morris, Nicholas Grohe; Design Collaborators: Primary Group; Architects: Wallace, Floyd, Associates; Engineer/Project Management: Bechtel/Parsons Brinckerhoff.

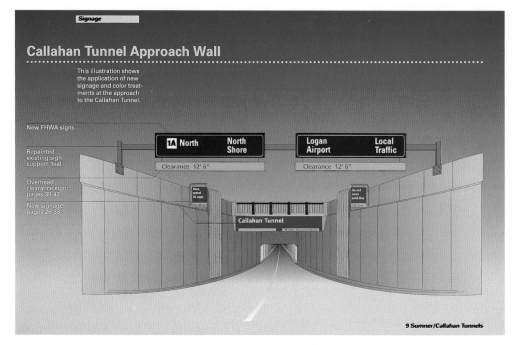

Signage

Callahan Tunnel Approach Wall

This illustration shows the application of new signage and color treatments at the approach to the Callahan Tunnel.

New FHWA signs

Repainted existing sign support: teal

Overhead clearance sign: pages 39-42

New signage: pages 26-33

1A North — North Shore

Clearance 12' 6"

Logan Airport — Local Traffic

Clearance 12' 6"

Max. speed 35 mph

Do not cross solid line

Callahan Tunnel

9 Sumner/Callahan Tunnels

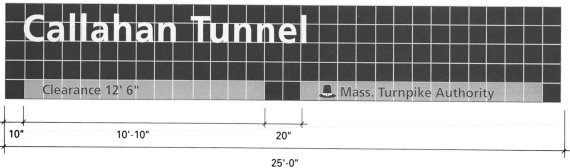

Callahan Tunnel

Clearance 12' 6" — Mass. Turnpike Authority

10" — 10'-10" — 20"

25'-0"

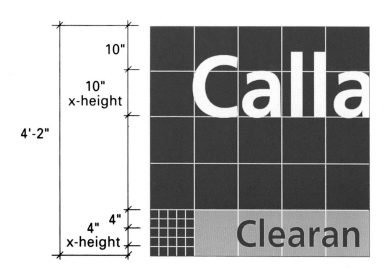

4'-2" — 10" — 10" x-height — 4" 4" x-height

Calla

Clearan

For a renovation of the Sumner Callahan Tunnels in Boston, Two Twelve developed a complete program of environmental graphic design standards, including signage and architectural color treatments. Bright colors serve as a counterpoint to the neutral shades of the existing tunnel environment. Client: Massachusetts Turnpike Authority; Design Directors: David Gibson, Douglas Morris; Designer: Nicholas Grohe; Design Collaborators: Primary Group.

The Trump Shuttle Air Terminal signage system combines conventional, static signs with dynamic, electronic displays for this air carrier providing service to Boston, New York and Washington, D.C. Signage includes passenger waiting areas, ticket counter stations and gate areas. The project was completed in five weeks to insure smooth operations during a transitional retrofit following new ownership. Client: The Trump Organization; Design Director: David Gibson; Designers: Jose Delano, David Peters; Architects: Clark Harris Tribble & Li; Photographer: Jennifer Levy.

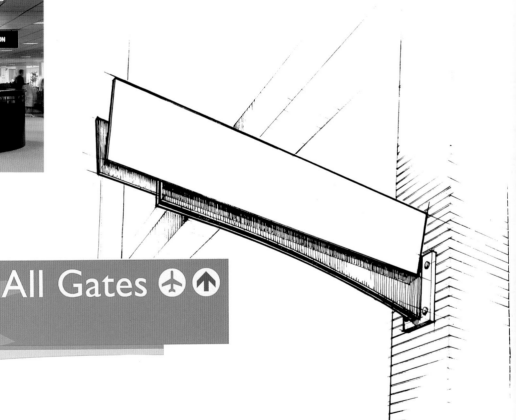

Comprehensive communications system, including conventional and electronic signs, for the new T.F. Green Airport in Rhode Island. The shape of mountings complements the buildings' curved roofs. Airplane and bus/car symbols designate departure and arrival pathways. Client: Rhode Island Department of Transportation; Design Directors: David Gibson, Douglas Morris; Designers: Nicholas Grohe, Ben Goodman; Architects: Howard Needles Tammen & Bergendoff.

Clifford Selbert Design, Inc.

2067 Massachusetts Ave.
Cambridge, MA 02140
617/497-6605

Principal:
Clifford L. Selbert

Year Founded: 1982
Size of Firm: 20

Sign system for
CambridgeSide Galleria
Parking Facility, for New
England Development,
Cambridge, Massachusetts.
Designers: Robin Perkins,
Clifford Selbert;
Fabricator: Design
Communications;
Photographer:
Peter Lewitt.

Principal Clifford L. Selbert.

Billboard campaign
for KIIS FM, Los Angeles,
California. Designers:
Robin Perkins, Clifford
Selbert; Photographer:
Jonathan Exley; Printer:
Outdoor Posters, David
Staley, Reno Nevada;
Metromedia, Los Angeles.

Promotional T-shirts for
WXKS FM, Boston,
Massachusetts. Designer:
Lynn Riddle.

Key Clients:
AGFA, Alessi,
Boston Redevelopment
Authority, Brigham &
Women's Hospital,
Converse,
Fidelity Investments,
Graham Gund and
Associates, Hardy
Holzman Pfeiffer
Associates, Harvard
Community Health Plan,
Harvard University,
Lotus Development
Corporation,
National Park Service,
New England
Medical Center,
New York
Botanical Garden,
WXKS FM Boston.

Clifford Selbert Design, Inc.

Mailbox design
for The Markuse
Corporation, Woburn,
Massachusetts. Designer:
Clifford Selbert.

Clifford Selbert, trained as a landscape architect at Rhode Island School of Design, brings an urban-scale vision to all his projects–even those that might, in ordinary circumstances, simply call for "graphic design." When asked to create a promotion for the City of New Haven enticing businesses to move to the city, Selbert flatly refused to produce the usual brochures and folders generated by municipalities across the country. Instead, his firm assembled an enticing box of New Haven souvenirs, each housed in a smaller package grouped around a central green cube signifying the city's central square. Selbert's urban vision comes from hands-on experience: for five years he worked for the City of Providence as a "one-man band in charge of 100 parks." There he designed parks, park furniture, sign systems and print promotions. Selbert's Cambridge-based company offers landscape architecture among its services–an unusual depth of expertise even for an environmental design firm. Selbert summarizes his attitude as "design activism," marked by a commitment to making "design as if it matters." He affirms design as a powerful force that touches people's everyday lives, and nowhere more evident than in the creation and interpretation of parks and cities.

Exterior sign for Editel
Boston, Inc., Boston,
Massachusetts.
Designers: Linda Kondo,
Clifford Selbert;
Photographer: Anton
Grassl; Fabricators:
Design Communications,
Ltd., TIR Systems Ltd.

Sign for Joie de Vivre,
Cambridge, Massachusetts.
Designers: Robin Perkins,
Clifford Selbert;
Fabricators: Wood &
Wood (Sparky Potter);
Photographer:
Anton Grassl.

**Clifford Selbert
Design, Inc.**

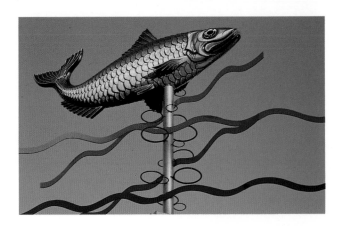

*Masterplan, landscape architecture
and environmental graphics for Seven
Hills Park, for the City of Somerville,
Massachusetts. Seven Hills Park is
a community landmark; the graphics
and sculptural elements refer to
historical places, sites, and areas of
commerce. Designers: Robin Perkins,
Clifford Selbert; Fabricator:
Amidon Sign & Co. (Steve Purcell);
Photographer: Anton Grassl.*

*Environmental graphics standards
for Harvard Community Health Plan,
Brookline, Massachusetts. Sites here:
Burlington, Quincy and Brookline,
Massachusetts. Designers:
Clifford Selbert, Boyd Morrison,
Linda Kondo, Jon Straggas;
Photographer: Anton Grassl; Fabricator:
Advanced Signing, Back Bay Sign.*

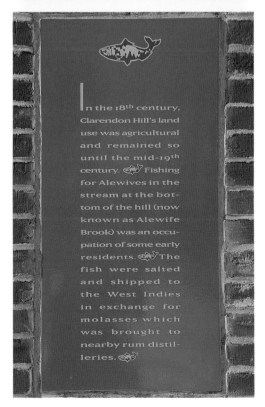

In the 18th century, Clarendon Hill's land use was agricultural and remained so until the mid-19th century. Fishing for Alewives in the stream at the bottom of the hill (now known as Alewife Brook) was an occupation of some early residents. The fish were salted and shipped to the West Indies in exchange for molasses which was brought to nearby rum distilleries.

**Clifford Selbert
Design, Inc.**

"Simple New Approach to Checking" (SNAPP) gateway sign for Bank of New England incorporates architectural motifs of hanging tetrahedrons and pyramids, which invite clients into an interior that evokes structural as well as financial stability. Designers: Linda Kondo, Melanie Lowe, Boyd Morrison, Clifford Selbert.

Sign for Lyons Group Management for Zanzibar, a popular Boston nightclub, was designed within the vibrant urban context, while enhancing its visibility. Designer: Robin Perkins; Fabricator: Design Communications.

Environmental graphics for The Browne Fund, a trust founded for the "benefit and adornment" of Boston, for the City of Boston and the Browne Fund, Boston, Massachusetts. Here, etched bronze for the Monument Square site and porcelain enamel for Tai Tung Village. Designers: Linda Kondo, Clifford Selbert; Photographers: Anton Grassl, the Slide Center; Fabricators: Design Communications, Ltd., Winsor Porcelain Enamel Display, Inc.

*In-store banners, package design,
press conference invitation, and point-
of-purchase display for Converse, Inc.
Designers: Linda Kondo, Melanie Lowe,
Clifford Selbert; Photographers: Peter
Rice, Francine Zaslow; Fabricators:
Branded Apparel and Incentives,
Steve Mahoney, Altec Plastics, Inc.*

Product display gives
at-a-glance choice of
different styles of this
icon of American shoes.

**Clifford Selbert
Design, Inc.**

Sign System (identity, information, and wayfinding) for New York Botanical Garden, New York, integrates floral illustration throughout to signify landmarks for particular areas of the gardens. Designers: Linda Kondo, Clifford Selbert; Architect: Hardy Holzman Pfeiffer Associates; Photographer: Anton Grassl; Fabricators: Design Communications, Ltd., Computer Image Systems; Illustrators: Paul Ritscher, Bruce Hutchison, Melanie Lowe, Daniel Craig.

Botanical
illustrations.

Main entrance detail.

Kiosk at Azalea Way
includes detailed "bird's-
eye view" map.

Commemorative
book and map
of gardens.

Banner at
main entrance.

Donovan and Green

71 Fifth Avenue
New York, NY 10003
212/725-2233

Principals:
Michael Donovan
Nancye Green

Year Founded: 1974
Size of Firm: 30

Nancye Green and Michael Donovan, principals of Donovan and Green.

Rockefeller Center

Buildings

1 **RCA Building**
30 Rockefeller Plaza
2 **RCA Building West**
1250 Avenue of the Americas
3 **AMAX Building**
1270 Avenue of the Americas
4 **Radio City Music Hall**
1260 Avenue of the Americas
5 **The Associated Press Building**
50 Rockefeller Plaza
6 **International Building**
630 Fifth Avenue
7 **International Building North**
636 Fifth Avenue
8 **Palazzo d'Italia**
626 Fifth Avenue
9 **British Building**
620 Fifth Avenue
10 **La Maison Française**
610 Fifth Avenue
11 **Manufacturers Hanover Trust Building**
500 Fifth Avenue
12 **One Rockefeller Plaza**
13 **Eastern Air Lines Building**
10 Rockefeller Plaza
14 **Simon & Schuster Building**
1230 Avenue of the Americas

Elevator floor signage, directory information, and directional signs for Rockefeller Center. The program reflects the landmark's art deco detailing. Materials include brass, glass and plexiglass. Partner-in-Charge: Michael Donovan; Project Team: Eileen Boxer, Louis Scrima; Fabricator: The Other Sign Company.

Painted plywood construction barricade banners, for Republic National Bank. The banner colors changed with the seasons. Partner-in-Charge: Michael Donovan; Fabricator: The Other Sign Company.

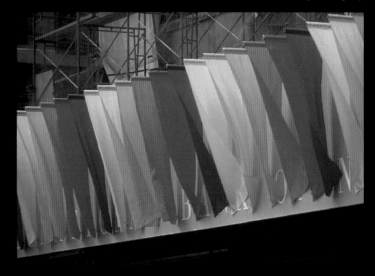

Key Clients:
American Center
for Physics,
American Express,
Corning, Inc.,
Herman Miller, Inc.,
Liberty Science Center,
Linpro,Olympia &
York Properties,
Peabody Museum
of Salem, Raychem,
Rockefeller Center
Development
Corporation,
The Ronald Reagan
Presidential Library,
3M,Tishman Speyer
Development
Corporation,
TRW,United States
Olympic Committee,
UPS.

Donovan and Green

Donovan and Green's work is characterized not only by its strong visual presence and its clear, confident delivery of information, but also by the rich interpretive skills the firm uses to reveal the ideas and personality that animate a company, institution, or individual. The designers immerse themselves in the history and philosophy surrounding a given project before arriving at design solutions. Ambitious exhibition projects, such as The Ronald Reagan Presidential Library and the Corning Glass Headquarters in New York, have drawn on Donovan and Green's ability to create complete environments that convey its clients' interests through the compelling tools of education and entertainment.

Peabody Museum of Salem, Asian Export Art Wing is designed to showcase over 10,000 pieces of art. Designs for entrance, pavilion galleries and display cases include extensive visual and graphic interpretive materials such as lacquered wood, plexiglas, and silkscreens incorporating traditional Chinese, Japanese, and Indian motifs. Partner-in-Charge: Michael Donovan; Associate Partner: Susan Berman; Project Team: Robert Henry, Lori Hom; Fabricator: Rathe Productions; Photographer: Wolfgang Hoyt.

The Ronald Reagan Presidential Library exhibition areas were designed to incorporate a number of multimedia experiences with interactive and passive exhibits mutually reinforcing each other. Lighting systems and multimedia hardware were specified with consideration given to their reliability and ease of maintenance over a long period of time. The total environment was designed to be comfortable, friendly, and accessible. In the "Voices of Freedom" gallery, cases contain artifacts and photos from individuals persecuted for their political and/or religious beliefs.

A steel-paneled wall lists names of dissidents from around the world, as well as world events since 1988. Partner-in-Charge: Nancye Green; Associate Partner: Susan Berman; Project Team: Alexis Cohen, Alan Ford, Gabrielle Goodman, Robert Henry, Adrian Levin, Susan Myers, Patrick Nolan, Allen Wilpon; Fabricators: Peerless Woodworking/ The Larkworthy Group, Signs and Decal; Photographer: Nick Merrick/ Hedrich Blessing.

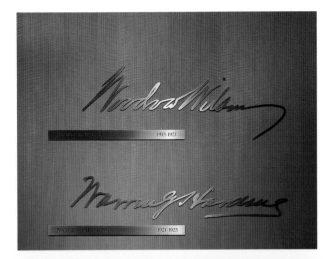

"The Hall of Presidents" gallery features cut-out bronze signatures of the 39 presidents preceding Reagan. Anigre wood veneer walls form the closure. Reagan's signature is placed on a back-lit glass wall in which the presidential seal is sandblasted.

Worldwide Plaza interior and exterior signage program incorporates carved entrance lettering and traditional typography. Partner-in-Charge: Michael Donovan; Associate Partner: Susan Berman;

Project Team: Alexis Cohen, Robert Henry, Lori Hom; Fabricator: Signs and Decal; Photographer: Austin Hughes.

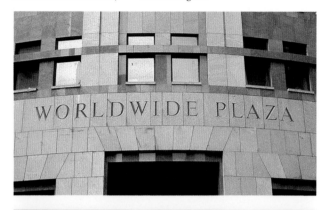

United States Olympic Committee Traveling Exhibition emphasizes visitor interactivity. Entry ramp and map/rail display exterior graphic panels illustrating Olympic events. Partner-in-Charge: Michael Donovan;

Associate Partner: Patrick Nolan; Project Team: Carrie Berman, Dana Christensen, Alexis Cohen, Ina Gallon; Fabricator: CMS Corporate Graphics; Photographer: Wolfgang Hoyt.

Etched and filled bronze framework of directory sign echoes architectural motifs.

Herman Miller Pavilion,
Marketing/Education Center in Zeeland,
Michigan reiterates the company's
"invention" of modern office systems.
Pavilion space includes multitiered
"Spanish Steps" for seating display;
product display alcoves and freestanding
graphic exhibit panels that convey
specific product and program
information. Partner-in-Charge:
Michael Donovan; Project Team:
Eileen Boxer, Dana Christensen, Gwen
Wilkins; Fabricator: Displaymakers;
Photographer, Nick Merrick/
Hedrich Blessing.

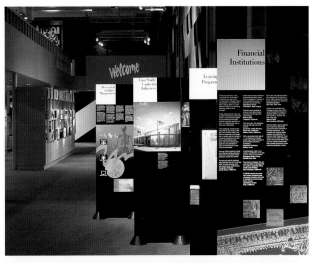

CORNING

Corning Incorporated
Steuben Offices

White light was focused on dichroic filters, optical mirrors, and prisms which were programmed by computer in a constantly changing palette.

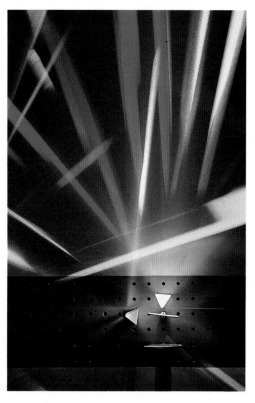

Properties of glass and light were the design foundation for the Corning Corporate Headquarters exhibition in New York. Utilizing basic optical principals and state-of-the-art technology reflecting Corning's history and advancements in fiber optics communications, an engaging mural of spectral "painting" greets visitors.
Partner-in-Charge: Michael Donovan;
Project Associate: Allen Wilpon;
Fabricator: Maltbie Associates;
Photographer: Wolfgang Hoyt.

By Wim Crouwel

Environmental Graphics: Heaven and Hell

Discussions on environmental graphics always make me somewhat querulous. Look what we've done to our cities. We have messed up the whole visual environment with advertising graphics and signage.

Wouldn't it be best to get rid of it all? Cleaning the landscape and the streets of signposts, advertising, shop signs, billboards and street-furniture would possibly be a great service to mankind. Imagine the moment that we took away the whole lot and were able to again see the facades of buildings; to look at the first and second storeys the way the architects designed them to be seen. Think about the joy going through a landscape without flashy monuments for inns and hotels, without typographic triumphal arches, telling us which way to go. It would be heaven: aesthetic, clean and empty, with no persuasive diversions.

At the same time, I wonder greatly if this is what we really want. The burden of our cultural heritage makes us very nervous now and then. However nice it seems, this heavenly clean outlook is to a great extent very unrealistic. I also see some boredom and uneasiness. I'm afraid such a virginal situation will almost certainly lead to an uninformed society, one that in the end is not even able to communicate. Then there will be real cleanliness—and emptiness all around!

The reality is that people have always wanted and needed to communicate; and whether we like it or not, this information society always needs more and better carriers of this information for a higher level of understanding. Such a process never develops along harmonious lines. On the contrary, the amount of unsuccessful, distracting and misleading information carriers is always larger than the serious ones. In this end-period of post-modernism, where architecture changes from an abstraction of an attitude to a profanely articulated meaning, this very architecture is entering the domain of signage and advertising.

Especially in the last decades society has become very complex, and our man-made visual environment is a clear reflection of this complexity. There is a constant conflict of interests. Aesthetic order and clarity are in a continuous battle with confusion and non-communication. Into the battle comes the designer, as a warrior at the side of good sense, trying to find new strategies that will lead to victory. The victory of a human, harmonious visual environment, away from the existing muddle; an environment where we are well informed and can find our way, and where all communication channels are wide open.

Is it understandable that I—as one of those warriors—sometimes wish to be a mighty general, at least able to clear the whole environment from superfluous and ugly obstacles?

Wim Crouwel was born in Groningen, The Netherlands, where he studied design at the Academy of Applied Arts. He was a co-founder and a partner of Total Design, in Amsterdam and has held faculty positions at the University of Technology in Delft and Erasmus University in Rotterdam. His award-winning work is represented internationally in major design collections and museums. In 1989 he was conferred an Officer of the Most Excellent Order of the British Empire (OBE).

Communication or chaos? A confusion of competing signage on a street in Amsterdam attests to the necessity of balancing a well-designed visual environment with our information-hungry culture.

168

**Chermayeff &
Geismar Inc.**

15 East 26th Street
New York, NY 10010
212/532-4499

Principals:
Ivan Chermayeff
Thomas Geismar
John Grady
Steff Geissbuhler

Associates:
Keith Helmetag
Cathy Schaefer

Year Founded: 1960
Size of Firm: 35

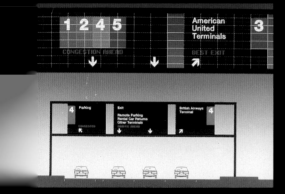

Roadway sign guidelines
for JFK 2000 Airport.
Pei Cobb Freed &
Partners, Architects.

Left to right: Helmetag, Geissbuhler, Geismar, Schaefer, Chermayeff, Grady.

At IBM building, moving light
bars indicate direction and
location of each elevator.
Edward Larrabee Barnes/John
M.Y. Lee, Architects.

Subway concourse
signs and murals at a
Lexington Avenue
station in midtown
New York. Edward
Larrabee Barnes/John
M.Y. Lee, Architects.

Building identification
for the Museum of
Contemporary Art,
Los Angeles.
Arata Isozaki, Architect.

Key Clients:
American Republic
Insurance,
Basketball Hall of Fame,
Best Products,
Boston Properties,
Charles Square,
Chase Manhattan Bank,
Children's Museum
of Manhattan,
Gemini Consulting,
Hudson River Museum,
IBM,
JFK Airport,
Knoll,
Museum of
Contemporary Art,
Los Angeles,
Mobil,
Museum of Modern Art,
New York,
National Park Service,
New England Aquarium,
New School for
Social Research,
Ohio Center,
Philip Morris,
Port Authority of
NY & NJ,
St. Louis
Children's Zoo,
Time Warner,
Tishman Speyer,
U.S. Information
Service,
Washington Dulles
Airport Authority.

Chermayeff & Geismar Inc.

Lion drinking
fountain for St. Louis
Children's Zoo.

Chermayeff & Geismar Inc.,
founded in 1960, shaped the
emerging field of institutional
graphics by exploring and
expanding the modernist ideal of
design as a multidisciplinary activity that
encompasses all aspects of public image, from
logotypes and business communications to
architectural environments. While the strategies
of corporate communication forged by
Chermayeff & Geismar Inc. have been widely
adopted throughout the design profession, the
firm has repeatedly surpassed its own standards,
maintaining a sense of humor and a spirit
of artistic invention and entrepreneurial change
over more than three decades, in work for
clients that include some of the world's most
influential cultural and commercial institutions.

One of 12 wallhangings
commissioned by
Philip Morris, Cabarrus
County, North Carolina.
This 10' x 40' sampler is
made of 324 traditional
patterns and is one of
the world's largest quilts.

Six-story high Christmas
trees fabricated of solar
mylar film were installed
in one day for Rose
Associates at One
Financial Center, Boston.

Chermayeff & Geismar Inc.

Neon cafeteria mural and exterior sculptures designed for Philip Morris, Richmond, Virginia. In the cafeteria, colored neon behind raised wall sections reflects soft pastel colors. In a reflecting pool, geometric forms continue the theme in three dimensions. Davis, Brody & Associates, Architects.

Life-size figures of painted laser-cut steel for the Knoll showroom in Chicago.

Five-story high ceramic tile mural for the Osaka "Ring of Fire" Aquarium in Japan. Below, a black light mural of shark silhouettes for the New England Aquarium, Boston. Cambridge Seven Associates, Architects.

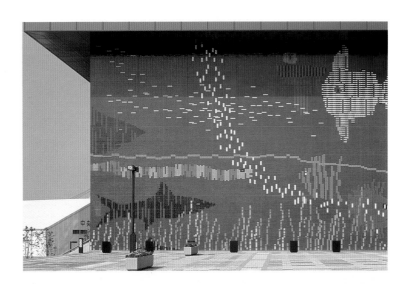

**Chermayeff &
Geismar Inc.**

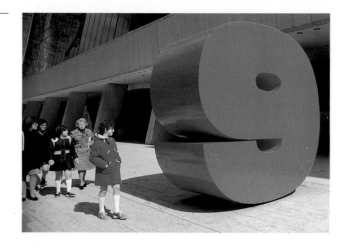

Street sculpture for
9 West 57th Street,
New York City.
Skidmore, Owings &
Merrill, Architects.

Retail store signage
for Best Products.

Basketball players
as identity for the
Basketball Hall of
Fame, Springfield,
Massachusetts.
Cambridge Seven
Associates, Architects.

Headquarters of
Time Warner,
New York City.

Identity pylons
serve as sculpture:
Charles H. Yalem
Children's Zoo,
St. Louis; Philip Morris,
Richmond, Virginia;
The Hudson River
Museum, Yonkers,
New York; University
of Pennsylvania,
Philadelphia.

Exterior sign and wave
mural for the New
England Aquarium,
Boston. Cambridge Seven
Associates, Architects.

The Urban Treehouse
at the Sussman
Environmental Center
of the Children's
Museum of Manhattan.
A multi-level permanent
steel structure houses
interactive exhibits.

Collages of recycled
found objects are signs
for can, cardboard, and
garbage disposal areas
at Gemini Consulting,
Morristown, New Jersey.

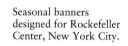

Seasonal banners designed for Rockefeller Center, New York City.

Painted construction barricades and retail space windows combine advertising and identity. Locations include two on Madison Avenue and 15 East 26th Street in New York City and Brickell Avenue, Miami.

Cato Design Inc.

254 Swan Street
Richmond, 3121
Australia
613/429-6577

Offices located in:
Melbourne, Auckland,
Perth, Singapore,
Sydney and Tokyo.

Principal: Ken Cato

Year Founded: 1970
Size of Firm: 56

Corporate identity for
Rott Nest Lodge, a
popular resort on an
island off the coast of
western Australia.
Designer: Ken Cato.

Ken Cato, principal of Cato Design Inc.

Corporate identity for
MFP Australia,
Adelaide. The prime
objective of this urban
and community
development is to ensure
Australia's successful
participation in
industries that will
be dominant in the
21st century.
Designer: Ken Cato.

Key Clients:
Australian Airlines,
BHP Australia,
Commonwealth Bank,
Coles Myer
Johnson & Johnson,
Multi-Function
Polis Australia,
Museum of Victoria,
National Dairies,
Phillip Morris,
Swan Brewery,
Tupperware Japan.

Cato Design Inc.

 Cato Design Inc., over its two-decade history, has emerged as both a big fish in a little pond and a big fish in a big pond. The firm is one of the largest and most successful design offices in Australia, a country with a tiny, late-blooming design community. Cato Design is also a significant player in the vast and fertile economic ecosystem of the Pacific Rim, with clients in New Zealand, Singapore, Tokyo, Hong Kong and Los Angeles. The clean, confident internationalism of the firm's work reflects the ongoing currency of the corporate modernism that crystallized out of the social upheavals and artistic experiments of the European avant-garde. The modernist ideal of a complete design environment–graphics, architecture, interiors, products and even fashion–is evident in principal and founder Ken Cato's commitment to environmental design: "We conceive total visual solutions. Everything that a company produces is designed. It's a matter of whether you choose to control it or not."

Symbol for Jurong Bird Park, Singapore. The park is a major tourist attraction and home to 3,500 birds. Banners for the front entrance feature characteristics of various bird species. Identity application also included uniforms, calendars and stationery. Designer: Ken Cato.

Program guide for Melbourne International Festival of the Arts. An enduring symbol of the arts, the mask is the focal point and identity of this piece.
Designer: Ken Cato.

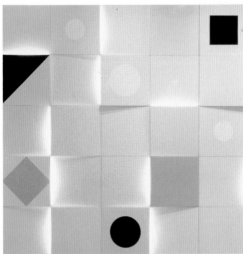

Design of Tabaret entertainment outlet for Totalizator Agency Board, Melbourne. Electronic computerized sporting games are the basis of the Tabaret operation. Designer: Ken Cato.

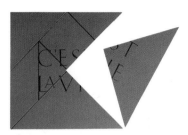

Corporate identity for C'est La Vie, a Japanese land developer committed to creating harmony between man and the environment. The triangles are an executive puzzle based on the Chinese tangram. Designer: Ken Cato.

MELBOURNE
1996

Product and promotional exhibit for Laminex Industries, Australia's leading manufacturer of decorative interior building surfaces. A new product launch was designed as a walk-through sculptural exhibition complete with a poster-size 3-D invitation. Designer: Ken Cato.

Symbol for 100th Anniversary Olympic Games, designed for the Melbourne Olympic Candidature bid for the 1996 games in Australia. The flame incorporates the five colors of the Olympic rings. A set of human figures in athletic poses was developed to give interest to the visual identity. Designer: Ken Cato.

Graphic identity and
signage system for
Rowland Food Hall,
Melbourne. The signage
and graphics are etched
onto glass panels.
Designer: Chris Perks.

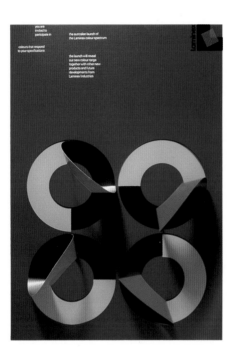

Poster-size 3D invitation
for Laminex Industries
product promotion.

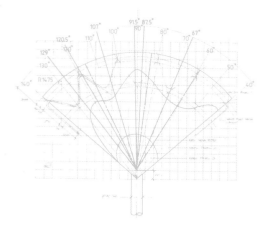

Graphic identity for
Pidemco Land Ltd.,
Singapore. The identity
is based on an isometric
representation of the
city grid and represents
the company's and the
city's real estate growth.
Designer: Ken Cato.

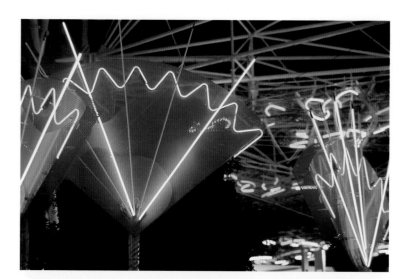

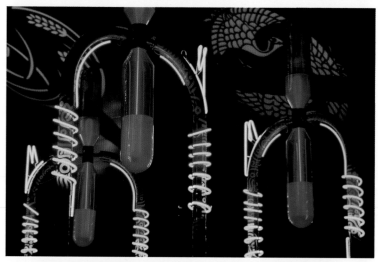

Identity for Foodtown
Supermarkets, Ltd., New
Zealand. Foodtown was
the first "lifestyle" super-
market in New Zealand.
It is warm, friendly,
spacious and airy.
Interiors are neutral to
allow the products to
be prominent.
Designer: Ken Cato.

Design for the World Expo, Brisbane.
A series of banners and hoardings
enhanced the streetscape of the site.
The neon ceiling, a vast "painting in
light," was animated by a computerized
program. Neon ground structures
were designed to link the ceiling to the
walkways below. Designer: Ken Cato.

Meeker & Associates, Inc.

1865 Palmer Avenue
Larchmont, NY 10538
914/834-1904

Principal:
Donald T. Meeker

Associates:
Peter Reedijk
Harriet Spear

Year Founded: 1985
Size of Firm: 5

Seated left to right Peter Reedijk, Harriet Spear, and Donald Meeker.

The symbols signs project for the Corps of Engineers includes 109 symbols in formats appropriate for recreation, prohibition, warning and highway signage. Used throughout all public park lands nationwide, the system updates the existing National Park Service symbols to create a visually consistent, legible program designed in the style of the D.O.T./AIGA symbol sign system.

Client: U.S. Army Corps of Engineers, with additional funding from the National Endowment for the Arts and support from the National Park Service and the Society for Environmental Graphic Designers; Designers: Donald Meeker, Peter Reedijk, Paul Singer and Elke Zimmer, with Dr. Irwin Siegel, NYU Medical Center, School of Ophthalmology.

Key Clients:
Boise Cascade
Corporation,
Champion International
Corporation,
Corps of Engineers
Evergreen Aviation
Corporation,
Marble Collegiate
Church,
Metropolitan Opera
Association,
National Park Service
Oregon Economic
Development
Department,
Port of Portland,
Rochester International
Airport,
United States
Forest Service,
Whitney Museum of
American Art,
Willamette University,
Xerox Realty
Corporation.

Meeker & Associates, Inc.

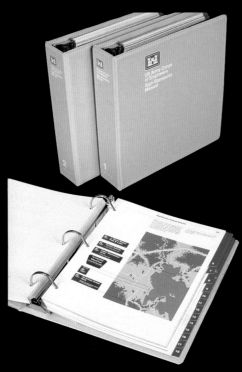

The Corps of Engineers sign program was developed over a multi-year process of planning and design, and included development of a management program for implementation. The program is documented in a two-volume standards manual with a project identification sign (right).

 Meeker & Associates is a firm noteworthy for sheer breadth of impact on the American landscape. Their design of a 4,500-recreation site nationwide sign system for the Corps of Engineers is the largest federal design implementation program in the U.S. Other wide-ranging projects include the development of a new system of national recreational symbols and the design of new sign standards for all U.S. navigable rivers and waterways. For Oregon the firm is designing the first statewide travel information sign program that includes historic and interpretive signs on special routes throughout the state, and in the Sierras they are designing a new sign system for Yosemite National Park. The firm is also heavily involved in research, consulting with the Pennsylvania Transportation Institute to improve American highway signs. Such expansive projects require intensive management as well as a rigorous logic for both design and implementation.

The sign system for the Columbia River Gorge National Scenic Area was designed to adapt to three different levels of road systems. The system integrates indigenous geologic and structural elements such as columnar basalt and redwood panels formed in the traditional arch shape. Graphics are routed and stained, with porcelain enamel inserts. Designers: Donald Meeker, Peter Reedijk; Landscape Architects: Doug Macy, David Vala, Walker & Macy Landscape Architects.

Entry portal cardboard mockup of a city identification sign (above). The sign panels integrate a classic Copperplate alphabet with a color system based on the area's four climate zones.

The road signs for the Oregon Sign System are different from common traffic signs and are used to guide visitors to public facilities and attractions managed by state, local and federal agencies. The sign hierarchy builds on a simple post and panel system with a common J-bolt connection assembly for accent. Each sign type has a unique assembly configuration. The program is being installed on 40 scenic and tour routes statewide with colors of sign selected for compatibility with each geographic area.

For the Oregon Department of Transportation Meeker & Associates developed a sign system that includes guides signs, tour route graphics and a program of historic and interpretive panels. Their design for a statewide system of maps, travel guides and visitor information centers are part of an extensive public works project to help enrich a visitor's experience with engaging graphics and an easy to use consistency statewide.
Designers: Donald Meeker, Peter Reedijk, Harriet Speare, Marianne Kelley; Landscape Architects: Doug Macy, David Vala, Walker & Macy Landscape Architects; Economic Planners: Dean Runyn, Chuck Nozicka, Dean Runyan & Associates; Historian and Interpretive Planner: Terence O'Donnell; Cartographers: William Loy, Jim Meacham, University of Oregon.

Triangular directional maps for the graphics system incorporates indigenous color and form with descriptive histories of selected sites. Interpretive panels are fabricated from both porcelain enamel and etched brass.

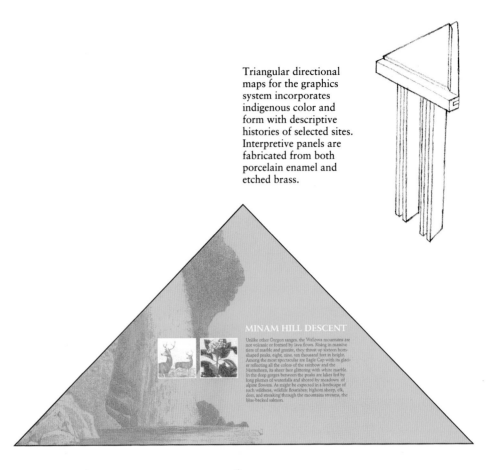

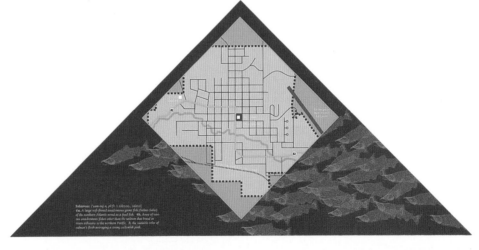

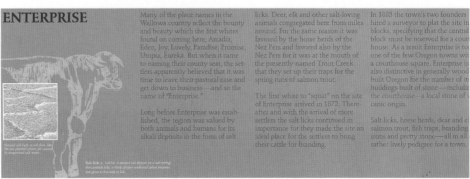

Clean, legible typography and bright color permit ease of directional access into the airport entry area with functionally finished back of assembly.

The Rochester International Airport has the amenities of a large facility on a smaller scale, in a relatively compact site. The roadway sign system developed by Meeker & Associates for Monroe County, New York makes the airport entry appear longer than it is, and also reflects the detailing of the terminal building architecture. Bright colors were selected to impart an upbeat quality in an area that is overcast much of the year. The sign panel system was scaled to the speed of approach, with five different sizes of square panels, including overhead entry signs, cantilever flags and double post ground mounted signs. Designers: Donald Meeker, Peter Reedijk; Consulting Engineers: Wayne Wegman and Gary Ponticello, Passero Associates; Structural Engineer: Eugene Avallone.

**Meeker &
Associates, Inc.**

Set in a beautifully
wooded site in southern
Connecticut, the signage
for Champion's Treetops
Corporate Conference
Center was designed to
identify the facility and
orient the first-time visitor
to parking and other
services. The signs are
fabricated from clear-heart
redwood, with routed
legends and finished with
gloss enamel. Designer:
Donald Meeker.

Each of the porcelain
enamel medallions is 26
inches across and is
illustrated in 12 colors.
Mounted on the
diamond, they have a
strong presence without
blocking sightlines
between the serving area
and the customer.

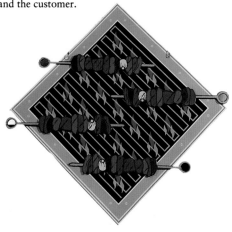

*For Champion International's new
Knightsbridge Corporate Campus
Cafeteria, nine decorative food
medallions were designed to identify
separate serving areas. Vibrant cartoon-
like illustrations are a graphic
complement to the soft burnished metals
of the cafeteria serving stations.
Meeker & Associates has also designed
for Champion a sign program for their
corporate headquarters and identity
signage for 240 manufacturing, mill,
administrative and timberland facilities,
as well as fleet graphics for trucks,
rail cars and other vehicles, production
line marking systems and product
packaging. Designers: Donald Meeker,
Peter Reedijk.*

For each of Champion's
paper sales offices
Meeker & Associates
designed and built
identification signs using
die-cut torn paper pulp.
Each is hand assembled
and uses the corporate
logo in a stacked,
variation on a theme

design. The graphic is
white, using shade and
shadow from spot
lighting to create a deep,
rich paper texture.
The 54" square panels
are placed in a box
frame with glass facings.
Designers: Donald
Meeker, Peter Reedijk.

As part of its 150th founding year commemoration, the campus sign program for Willamette University included freestanding directories, site maps, as well as guide and parking signs. The campus map and freestanding directories were manufactured from porcelain enamel and fabricated steel. Designers: Donald Meeker, Peter Reedijk, Doug Macy, Bo Nevue; Landscape Architects: Walker & Macy.

Street sign for Lansdowne New Town.

Xerox Realty Corporation's Lansdowne New Town is a development on the Potomac River near Leesburg, Virginia. Meeker & Associates worked with Richard Danne & Associates to develop a streetscape graphics plan for the 2,300-acre site, which included huge, conceptualized rope sculptures that serve to knit together and identify the project to passing motorists. The architectural drawings show the location of the ropes within the compound areas as it would appear upon approach. Designers: Donald Meeker, Peter Reedijk; Richard Danne & Associates; Landscape Architects: Cales Givens, HOH Landscape Architects and Planners.

Igarashi Studio

6-6-22 Minami-Aoyama
Minato-ku, Tokyo 107
Japan
03-3498-3621

Principal:
Takenobu Igarashi

Year Founded: 1970
Size of Firm: 9

Sculpture done to commemorate the 150th anniversary of the Kajima Corporation.

Sign for AIM Co., Ltd. is based on fundamental design shapes of circle, square and triangle.

Takenobu Igarashi, principal of Igarashi Studio.

Z, S, Y, O, N, A from the aluminum alphabet series of three dimensional letterforms. The sculptures extend the letterforms into both positive and negative directions, lending imagination to the graphic forms while maintaining legibility of the separate letters.

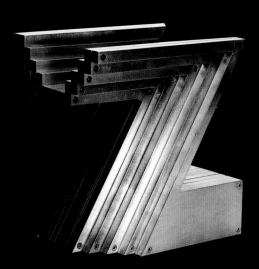

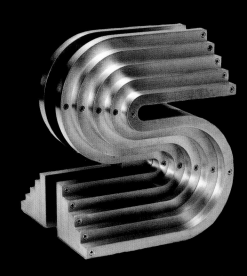

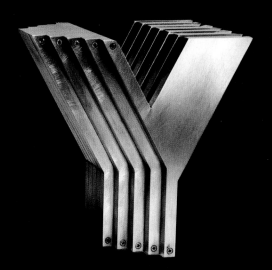

Igarashi Studio

Key Clients:
*Yamada Shomei
Lighting Co.,
Suntory Ltd.,
Honda Motor Co., Ltd.,
Kajima Corporation,
Kanazawa Institute
of Technology,
Keio University Library,
Nike Ltd.,
Nissan Infinity,
Oji Paper Co., Ltd.,
Parco, Ricoh Co., Ltd.,
The Square, Miwa SDI,
Suntory Hall,
Toranomon NN
Building,
Zanders Fienpapier.*

Stainless steel "3"
for head office of
Michael Peters Group,
London. Manufacturer:
Ralph Selby.

Directory sign sculpture
in front of Toranomon
NN Building, for Nippon
Insurance Company.
The two N's join at
right angles, creating
continuous surfaces for
listing directory
information. Architect:
Maki and Associates.

Takenobu Igarashi, for over 20 years,
has defined a concise and elegant
visual idiom that reflects the unique
culture of Japan while speaking
fluently to the international design
and business communities. Igarashi sees graphics,
products, sculpture and the environment as
sharing a fluid continuum, united by a single
challenge: to construct forms that are at once
functional and aesthetic. Igarashi began his
exploration of three-dimensional typography with
his alphabet sculptures of the late Seventies, which
study and reveal the abstract nature of letterforms
divorced from their utility as symbols. A similar
attitude is reflected in Igarashi's environmental
signage projects, where the monumental
abstraction of his alphabet sculptures merges
with the communicability of signs: the result is
functional sculpture. Igarashi embraces the
familiar maxim "form follows function," but not
in a formulaic, reductive manner. For Igarashi,
form is not a slave to function, but an ambitious,
demanding partner that continually questions
and redefines the limits of design problems.

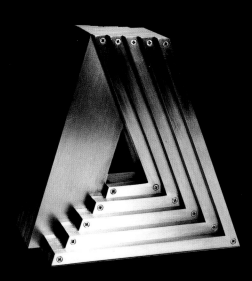

Aluminum sculpture
used for Nike Ltd.'s
180 running shoes
advertising promotion.

Wood sculpture celebrates the 55th anniversary of Tokyu Department Store.

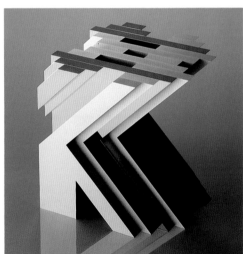

Kokuyo "K" sculpture is based on the company logo.

Based on the aluminum alphabet series, "O" sculpture for The Square; a stainless steel letterform with "floating" repeats on a granite base. Client: The Square.

Sculpture for
Suntory Hall.

For Suntory Ltd., Igarashi developed
a graphic identity based on the Chinese
character "hibiki," meaning echo,
reverberation, music, sound and space.
All of these characteristics are inherent
and reflected in the company's
philosophy. Suntory logo, entrance
sculpture and sign develop a single
geometric shape using repetitions of the
square as visual echos. Client: Suntory
Ltd.; Manufacturers: Dentsu, Inc.,
Nomura Kogei, Nelsa-Cobo; Materials:
Stainless steel with gold leaf, brass
with gold plate and bronze.

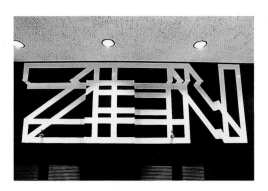

A wall graphic for Zen Environmental Design uses the company logo in a framework of its own letters. Interior Design: Shoei Yoh Design Office; Materials: Oil paint.

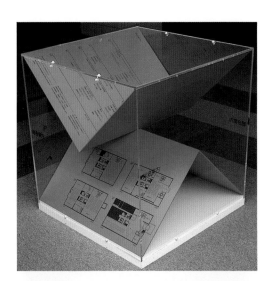

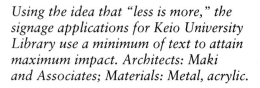

Using the idea that "less is more," the signage applications for Keio University Library use a minimum of text to attain maximum impact. Architects: Maki and Associates; Materials: Metal, acrylic.

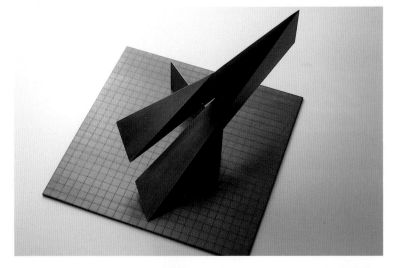

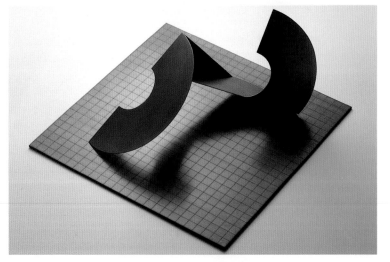

Letter "O", Mirror
Alphabet series.

Ori alphabet letterforms
"N", "P", "C", "Z".

In two series incorporating letterforms and illusory space, Igarashi draws attention to both symmetry of the forms and the graphic construction of the letters. In the Mirror Alphabet series, the letter "O" is formed from a single half-circle attached to a two-sided mirrored surface. On the reverse, the mirrored form reflects and creates the letter "V". The Ori Alphabet series of "hidden letters" challenge one's conceptions of letterform construction. Manufacturers: Sunrise Technique Co., Ltd., Nelsa-Cobo; Materials: Painted steel, aluminum, chrome-plated glass, mirror, ABS resin.

Letter "V", Mirror Alphabet series.

Index of Firms and Principals

BENEDUM
CIVIC CENTER LIBRARY

1230061283